INDIANS' REVENGE

including

A HISTORY OF THE YEMASSEE INDIAN WAR

1715 - 1728

by

William McIntosh, III

ISBN: 1-4392-4810-9
ISBN-13: 9781439248102

Visit www.booksurge.com to order additional copies.

CHAPTERS

FROM THE AUTHOR

I thank God that He gave me the ability and wherewithal to write this history of the Yemassee War. This is a war that today is virtually forgotten even though hundreds of white settlers and Indians died during a long, drawn out struggle. The Indians, for various reasons, had had enough of the English and sought revenge. It was bloody. The Yemassee War should be remembered for many reasons but primarily because it shows what happens when greed and cruelty rule. The book cover picture is the Beaufort River.

I thank my wife, Suzanne, for her inspiration and her hours of editing. This book is hers as much as it is mine.

Genealogy was the linchpin that launched this book. Thomas Hepworth, my great-grandfather eight generations back, who was Chief Justice of South Carolina from 1724 – 1727, like the Yemassee War, has been virtually forgotten. My learning about Hepworth's life led me to want to learn more about early life in colonial South Carolina. I was soon fascinated with the Yemassee War and quickly realized, no history of the war had ever been written that covered the war from its beginning in 1715 through its end in 1728. As far as I know, this book is the only one. I hope you enjoy reading this book as much as I enjoyed writing it.

THE BEGINNINGS

Ordinary people and those of a lower rank should be encouraged to marry Indians so it would be easier to convert the Indians to Christianity. For their efforts, each couple should receive some acreage and money from the public treasury, stated John Lawson, explorer of the Carolinas in 1700. He believed the Indians, after marriage and having forsaken the Indian lifestyle, would see whites were kind and just to them in all dealings and would forget their idolatry. Why the upper class was not included is not clear, but Lawson did not practice what he preached. Nor did any others follow his advice.

Through the years the whites were not kind and just in all dealings to the Indians. Because of that, the Indians, at times, would become a dangerous factor in the province. Thus the Indians were a major factor in the life of early South Carolina from the day in April 1670 when Charles Town, called Albermarle Point for a short time, was founded on the west bank of the Ashley River.

In 1663 eight men, who had been faithful to Charles II, had been given a grant to essentially develop the land between 31 and 36 degrees north and between the two oceans in return for annually paying the king twenty marks and giving him one-fourth of all gold and silver found. These men became the Lords Proprietors. Since an earlier grant had to be canceled, a revised charter was issued to the Lords Proprietors on June 30, 1665. The chief difference was that the southern boundary was changed to 29 degrees south so as not to include St. Augustine.[1]

One of the Lord Proprietors, Anthony Ashley-Cooper, Lord Shaftesbury, insisted on paying for Indian lands and on March 10, 1675, a deed was signed with the "Kassoes," that is the Kusso, for land between the Ashley, Stono and Edisto rivers. The Kussos were given certain clothes, hatchets, beads, etc. In 1684, in a series of treaties, the various coastal tribes from the Ashley to the Savannah River ceded to the proprietors their land as far inland as the mountains even though the land of these tribes did not extend past the coastal region. In exchange, the settlers were not to molest the Indians.[2]

Even with these initial good intentions, there were problems between whites and the Indians. "In 1671

---

1   Wallace, D.D *South Carolina A Short History* p. 24
2   Ibid. p. 34

the Kussos were accused of conspiring with Spanish Florida, enemies of South Carolina, and open war was declared. Friction with the Indians was inevitable."[3] Historian Verner Crane stated perhaps the Lords Proprietors were correct in speculating, "the wars were begun under specious pretexts, with the real aim of enslaving Indians. The first official recognition of Indian slavery came, apparently, at the conclusion of the campaign against the Kusso. In the beginning, Indian slavery was a means to secure volunteers for border defense, and for this purpose the Lords Proprietors sanctioned it. But soon it developed into a flourishing business, and later, into a cruelly efficient engine of encroachment upon the spheres of influence of France and Spain that were England's rivals in the south and west."[4]

Colonists complained about the Indians destroying their cattle and hogs during their hunts. Indians complained of unfair trade practices and of the destruction of their crops by the settlers' cattle and these caused reprisals. The Westoes murdered some Englishmen in 1673 and the Kussos did the same in 1674. South Carolina's policy was, "Unless prompt satisfaction was offered, punitive expeditions were sent out."[5]

---

3   Crane, Verner W. *The Southern Frontier 1670 – 1732*   p. 18
4   Ibid.
5   Ibid.

The Westoes, a tribe that lived along the lower Savannah River, was the most warlike of the coastal tribes. The other coastal tribes had welcomed the English in hopes they would offer some protection against this fierce tribe. In 1677 the Lords Proprietors declared only they could trade with the Westoes, Kashitas and the Spanish Indians beyond Port Royal, leaving the settlers the few settlement Indians with whom they could trade.

The settlement Indians were a group of Siouan tribes. These tribes, generally located between Charles Town and Port Royal included the Kusso, Kiawah, Stono, Wimbee, Combahee, Ashepoo, Wando, Sampa and Etiwan. The coastal Seewee were included even though they were north of Charles Town. There were less than 800 Indians in all these tribes.[6]

This trade monopoly claimed by the proprietors, plus the settlers desire to increase the Indian slave trade beyond the settlement Indians, eventually doomed the Westoes.

In 1677, after the Westoes murdered two settlers, they were refused entry into the settlement and had to bring any goods they wished to trade to certain plantations on the periphery. This order was

6   Johnson, David Lee *The Yamasee War* p. 33

renewed in 1680. Westoe attacks against the other Indian tribes continued which was the principal alleged reason for the war against the Westoe in 1680.[7]

"The Carolinians allied with the Savano Indians, a migrating group of Shawnee, recent newcomers, apparently, from west of the mountains." With their aid, the Westoes were defeated with little loss of life and at a low financial cost.[8]

"Whether or not the war arose out of the legitimate fears the planters had of the warlike Westoes or whether it was the desire to increase the Indian trade, is not known. The result of the war was the destruction of the proprietors' monopoly of the backcountry Indian trade. When peaceful intercourse was reestablished with the inland Indians, the trade was in the hands of a group of settlers."[9] However, this short war caused a period of peaceful relations with the Indians and the settlers that lasted until 1715.

The Lords Proprietors heard about the Westoe War at the end of 1680 or early 1681 when one Captain Strong arrived in England with letters from

---

7   Crane, Verner W. *The Southern Frontier*   p. 19
8   Ibid. p. 19 & 20
9   Fagg, Daniel W. Jr. *St. Giles: The Earl of Shaftesbury's Carolina Plantation* South Carolina Society Historical Society *Magazine* Vol. 71 p. 122

several Carolinians. The proprietors wrote back to the Carolinians that they did not know the cause of the war and wrote that if it was to protect the province, they approved, but if it was fought to "promote the advantage of particular persons," they did not approve. Looking after their financial interests, they reminded the Carolinians that "Peace is in the Interest of Planters." The colonists were chastised for not conveying the news sooner.[10]

It was in this letter to the Carolinians that the proprietors, perhaps, first put into writing the strategy of using allied Indians to protect South Carolina from attacks from the rear. They realized the Westoes were ravaged and they admitted the trade they had previously conducted with the Westoes had been only for monetary gain. The proprietors thought it might be smart to replace the Westoes with a "bold and warlike people" with arms and ammunition and other items useful to make them have a strong dependence upon the English. All the other Indians would be in awe. By protecting other tribes from this fierce tribe, other tribes would locate in English territory and all of these tribes would so terrify the Indians allied with the Spanish they would never attack South Carolina.[11]

---

10   British Public Records Office (BPRO) Roll I Vol. I p. 104
11   BPRO Roll I Vol. I p. 116/117

The Savanos, who now lived where the Westoes had lived, were considered, but it was the Yemassees who moved into the empty lower coastal area of South Carolina, with the permission of the government.[12] The Yemassees would replace the Westoes as protectors of the southern boundary.

The Yemassee were a Muskhogean tribe from north-central Georgia, who had migrated to Florida around the middle of the seventeenth century and eventually settled in the area of the upper St. Johns River.

Raids on Florida and St. Augustine in the 1680s by pirates and the British caused dissatisfaction between the Indians and the Spanish who offered little protection for the Indians. Also, there was an increasing demand for Indian foodstuffs and for Indian labor to help with the building of the stone fortress in St. Augustine. These actions caused the Yemassees to move to South Carolina.[13] Another source stated the Indians moved because the Spanish friars could not convert the "hardened infidels." In the winter of 1685 Spanish authorities executed several Yemassee. A sizeable number were also threatened with enslavement and sale in the West Indies. The Yemassees hated the Spanish

12   Wallace, D.D. *South Carolina A Short History* p. 8
13   Hann, John H. *The New History of Florida*   p. 79, 90 & 93 Edited by Michael Gannon

for thirty years.[14] Not all the Yemassees went to South Carolina. "A few pagans from a refugee Yemassee village," and some eight hundred Talimali, Chato and Escambe fled in 1704 across northern Florida because of rumors of an English attack on St. Augustine. Most of these Indians moved into Louisiana and settled near Mobile. The Yemassee were still there as late as 1711.[15]

Not everyone was thrilled with the arrival of the Yemassees into South Carolina. In 1685, Caleb Westbrook wrote from the short lived Scots settlement of Stuart Town on Port Royal Island that he feared there would be too many Indians arriving at one time and he was not certain if the Spanish had not sent them up to destroy South Carolina.[16]

In 1691, as part of their instructions to the governor of South Carolina, Philip Ludwell, the Lords Proprietors wrote they had thought for sometime it would be prudent to take all the Indians residing within 400 miles of Charles Town into English protection as subjects to the monarchy of England.

This policy worked well because the Indians preferred English goods. The Indians of South Carolina and in parts of what are now North Carolina, Tennessee

---

14   Johnson, David Lee *The Yamasee War* p. 34
15   Higginbotham, Jay *Old Mobile*   p. 191 & p. 462
16   BPRO Roll 1 Vol. 2 p. 8

and Georgia were so loyal to South Carolina that the province used the Indians to guard the back door. South Carolina totally relied upon Indians like the Cherokees to prevent an enemy, such as the French or the Indians allied with them, from attacking from the rear.

An early South Carolinian wrote in 1708 that the Chickasaws had no idea of any allegiance with anyone and were kept loyal only because the English traded much better items than the French could offer. A Chickasaw reported that the ladies of his tribe were very pleased to "look sparkling in the dances" wearing the clothes purchased from the English and would deeply regret it if that trade should end and they had to once again wear their old clothes made of painted buffalo calf skins.[17]

While the Lords Proprietors may have envisioned a 400 mile buffer zone, the Indian traders set no geographical limits to the area in which they would trade.

---

17   *Nairne's 1708 Muskhogean Journals* Edited with an Introduction by Alexander Moore p. 56/57

HENRY WOODWARD

Henry Woodward was not only the first to expand Indian trading to the edge of the 400 miles buffer zone but even beyond. The second "w" in Woodward's name is silent so the name is pronounced Woodard.[18] Woodward, from whom many are descended, is considered South Carolina's first white settler. Historian D.D. Wallace called him the founder of the Carolina Indian trade.

Woodward, a surgeon,[19] was born about 1646,[20] and arrived in South Carolina in 1666 with an expedition led by Robert Sandford, Esq., secretary and chief register of Clarendon County, North Carolina. A settlement had been established there in 1664. Sandford wanted to move his settlement further south and sailed in a three-ton vessel to Port

---

18 Mrs. Hume Guerard (Virginia) provided this information. See also BPRO Vol. I p. 26 where Woodward's name was spelled phonetically as "Woodard."
19 Woodward was a surgeon and is often referred to as Doctor Woodward. At that time surgeons were not educated in medical schools, but they learned when and where they could.
20 Woodward gave his age as 39 in May 1685. BPRO Roll I Vol. 2 p. 61

Royal[21] to explore it as a possible site. Woodward
decided to leave Sanford and to remain among
the Indians. Woodward's intention was possibly to
learn the language and customs of the Indians. That
knowledge would bode well for him later but before
he could put his knowledge to work, the Spanish
captured Woodward. He was then rescued from
St. Augustine by the English "Buccaneer" Robert
Searle. That led to him being cast up on the island of
Nevis during a hurricane. A later expedition, that left
England in 1669, was led by Colonel William Sayle
to establish a settlement in South Carolina. The
expedition stopped in Nevis and found Woodward,
who accompanied them from there.[22] Sayle was the
first governor of South Carolina.

Woodward went right to work in South Carolina
and obtained corn and other provisions from the
Indians and made treaties with them. Governor
Sir John Yeamans, South Carolina's third governor,
sent Woodward overland to Virginia in 1671 where
he made extended excursions into the interior in
search of precious metals.[23]

The Fundamental Constitution, the document Lord
Shaftesbury and his secretary, John Locke, drew up

---

21   Port Royal Island, South Carolina, is located 70 miles south of Charleston.
The towns of Beaufort and Port Royal are located on Port Royal Island.
22   Todd, John R & Hutson, Francis M. *Prince William's Parish and Plantations* p. 7
23   Barnwell, Joseph W. Article in *South Carolina Genealogies Vol. IV* p. 424

by which the province was to be governed, allowed each of the proprietors 12,000 acres. After Charles Town was securely settled, Lord Shaftesbury sent Andrew Percival, a merchant whose family in Dorset had been associated with the Ashleys for generations, as manager to launch his plantation. Percival, in turn, chose Henry Woodward for advice as to the best location for this endeavor. The plantation was established at the head of the Ashley River and by March 1675, 12,000 acres had been purchased from the Kussos. Percival had brought instructions to Woodward making him agent of the proprietor's Indian trade and he was to be paid one-fifth of the profits of whatever trade he carried on. He was also to make a trade treaty with the Westoe Indians and was to endeavor to open a secret trade with the Spanish in defiance of the Spanish governor's restrictions.[24] Woodward left a journal of his trip to the Westoes in 1674 that is printed in *Narratives of Early Carolina* edited by A.S. Salley, Jr.

In 1676 Woodward took the first substantial shipment of beaver furs, deerskins and less valuable bear, otter and fox furs to England. Even as agent of the proprietors, he had to pay £6 to cross the Atlantic on Shaftesbury's boat the *Edisto*.[25]

---

24   Fagg, Daniel W. Jr. *St. Gile's Seigniory* SCHS *Magazine* Vol. 71 p. 117 - 123
25   Ibid. p. 119

In 1685 Woodward and "half a dozen hardy fellows" were among the lower Creek Indians on the middle course of the Chattahoochee River. That was the farthest west that any Carolinian had ever ventured. This penetration created a crisis and the Spanish commander at Apalachee was soon on the march with a force of 250 men consisting of Christian Indians and Spaniards to save Spanish prestige and trade. Woodward withdrew from this, his last western trip, but he took back 150 Indians who had many skins to trade.[26]

Woodward married Mary Browne, widow of Robert Browne, and daughter of Colonel John Godfrey and his wife, Mary. Godfrey was one of the most notable men of the province. In 1672 Woodward was granted 150 acres as was everyone who had arrived in the original fleet. In 1678 he and his wife were granted 250 acres and on the same day, at the request of Lord Shaftesbury, he was granted 2,000 acres as a reward for his service. Woodward served on South Carolina's Grand Council,[27] as a deputy of Shaftesbury.[28] The Lords Proprietors paid Woodward £100 but in 1674 they said if he took

26   Wallace, D.D. *A Short History of South Carolina* p. 41 & 42

27   In the early years the Grand Council was the most important part of the government. A quorum consisted of the governor, three members appointed by the proprietors and three elected by the Assembly. D.D. Wallace *South Carolina A Short History* p. 33

28   Barnwell, Joseph W. Article in *South Carolina Genealogies* Vol. 4 p. 425 and Salley, A. S., Jr. *Warrants for Land in South Carolina Vol. I* p. 44, 148/149, 195/196, 201/202 and 210/211

any other items from the proprietor's stores, he would have to pay for them the same as any other person. Shaftesbury paid him an additional £20.[29] "Woodward died in late summer or early fall of 1686, as shown by Spanish records brought to light in recent years."[30]

Many South Carolinians would take part in the Indian trade as did Woodward. But only a few others had a vision for using the Indians to expand English territory in North America and for regulating the trade to prevent the abuses many traders heaped upon the Indians. Some of these men with a vision similar to Woodward's were John Barnwell, Thomas Nairne and Pryce Hughes.

29   Wallace, D.D. South Carolina *A Short History* p. 34
30   Todd, John R. & Hutson, Francis M. *Prince William's Parish and Plantations* p. 9 n. 6 and BPRO Roll I Vol. I p. 26

THE INDIANS IN OUR MIDST

The Reverend John Clayton wrote in 1687 of an interesting legend he learned during his sojourn in Virginia. He wrote Indian prophets had said one day bearded men[31] would come and take away their lands and there would be none of the original Indians remaining within a certain number of years. Clayton thought it was 150 years.[32] The visions of the Indian prophets became virtually true by 1790 when the population of the Indians east of the mountains in Virginia, North Carolina and South Carolina were reduced 95% to some 800 people.[33]

Diseases of the white man were to take a heavy toll on the Carolina Indians. Mrs. Affra Coming wrote to her sister in 1699 that smallpox had taken many lives, especially among the Indians. She stated a whole neighboring nation, which could mean a town or a village, was destroyed by smallpox except for five or six survivors who fled without burying

---

31   Indians did not have facial hair.
32   Marks, Geoffrey & Beatty, William K. *The Story of Medicine in America* p. 35
33   Axtell, James *The Indian's New South* p. 47

the dead.[34] Lawson also confirmed the Indians had lost many to "intestine Broils," but primarily to smallpox which "hath often visited them, sweeping away whole Towns."[35] In two centuries of contact with Europeans, nearly six of every seven Indians died of causes directly related to them.[36]

It was reported in 1708 that Indians closer to the Mississippi River were deserting towns and merging with other towns because of a decline in population due to firearms, smallpox and other European "distempers."[37] Newly discovered portable mirrors caused the naturally proud Cherokee Indians to die from smallpox in a strange way. During a 1738 epidemic, trader James Adair reported many of the Cherokees, who were always peeping into their mirrors, killed themselves upon seeing their disfigured faces. "Some shot themselves, others cut their throats, some stabbed themselves and others threw themselves with sullen madness into the fire."[38]

Nor did yellow fever spare Indians. In 1704 yellow fever struck the Indians near Mobile. According to a local source "the two villages of the Tomeh

---

34   Waring, Dr. J.I. *History of Medicine in South Carolina 1670 – 1825* p. 19

35   Lawson, John *A New Voyage to Carolina* p. 34 Edited with an Introduction by Hugh Talmage Lefler.

36   Waddell, Gene *Indians of the South Carolina Lowcountry* p. 14

37   *Nairne's 1708 Muskhogean Journals* Edited and Introduction by Alexander Moore p. 63

38   Axtell, James *The Indians' New South* p. 64/65

suffered more than any other native towns and the disease was blamed as being the main cause of their population declining from a total of eight hundred in 1704 to only eighty by 1724."[39]

In 1714, 800 Indians were living in South Carolina's Lowcountry between the Santee and the Combahee rivers, down from a peak of approximately 1,750 in 1576.[40] The population of a tribe could range from the Sewees with a population of 57 to the Etiwans with 240.

We seem to think of Indians as being stoic, but they had health problems not related to white men. A Dutch surgeon, who arrived in New Amsterdam in 1630 and traveled among the Iroquois, decided Indian medicine was not all "hocus pocus." He noted the Iroquois used sulphur to treat maladies, "but principally for their legs when they were sore from long marches."[41] Reverend John Clayton found the Indians had great success in curing wounds and sores. First they would suck the wound clean and then take something like a sweet weed, chew it and spit the juice onto the wound and finally apply salve-herbs binding it on with bark and silk grass.[42]

---

39   Higginbotham, Jay *Old Mobile* p. 194
40   Waddell, Gene *Indians of the South Carolina Lowcountry 1562 – 1751* p. 14
41   Marks, Geoffrey & Beatty, William K. *The Story of Medicine in America* p. 29
42   Ibid. p. 34

But disease alone did not decimate the numbers of Indians. Lawson reported the Sewees, who lived between Awendaw and the Santee River, realized the English traders among them were cheats. The Sewees had observed the arrival route of the English ships and decided England, where a better sort of people surely must live, lay but a short distance beyond the horizon. They decided they could receive higher prices for their pelts sold directly in England. The tribe, without a single dissenter, voted that some would build two large canoes for the journey while others would hunt to gather pelts. All of this was accomplished in great secrecy and when it was time to sail, only the "Old, Impotent and Minors" were left behind. As soon as the canoes were scarcely out of sight, a storm arose. It was presumed one canoe with its crew was lost at sea. The English ship captured the other canoe, the goods were confiscated and the Indians sold into slavery. This left fifty-seven surviving Sewees on shore.

Enslavement took a large toll on the Indian population. In 1708, the Spanish governor of Florida confessed the Indians allied with the English were raiding for slaves with impunity all the way to the Keys and in the past several years had carried off between 10,000 and 12,000 Indians.[43] Indians allied with the English were encouraged to war against those allied

---

43   Axtell, James *The Indians' New South* p. 37

with France or Spain to capture prisoners to be sold as slaves. It was a lucrative business.

Most Indians to be sold into slavery were exported because it was much easier for an Indian to escape in South Carolina and not be returned than a black. Even so by 1724, the peak of Indian slavery in South Carolina, there were 2,100 Indian men, women and children enslaved. The tax rate for an Indian slave was less than for a comparable black since they were of "much less value." After 1781 the institution and practice of Indian slavery in South Carolina became a rarity[44] because there were so few Indians left in South Carolina.

Who were these "savages" who were enslaved and cheated? Fortunately John Lawson left an invaluable description of the Carolina Indians and their customs following a seven-week trek through the Carolinas in 1700.

Lawson's account is very engaging, but not admired by one source that states, "Lawson's account of what he found in the Carolinas seems to be overly dramatic, and it is hard to believe in the primitive 'medicine' he described." The example given was that when one of Lawson's men became lame in one knee, treatment by the Indians "involved an

44   Snell, William R. *Indian Slavery in South Carolina 1671 – 1795* p. 101 & 117

instrument something like a comb which was made of split reed, with fifteen rattlesnake teeth. With these combs the Indian scratched the place where the lameness was until it bled. Then the lame knee was bathed with warm water and ground sassafras root was applied before it was bound. In a day or two the patient was well." This source continued, "It is a pity that John Lawson did not combine his flair for romantic description with the meticulous observation and devotion to investigatory detail that made Reverend John Clayton's account of the medical practice of the Virginia Indians an invaluable document."[45]

Be that as it may, Lawson seemed to like the Indians. He urged just and fair dealings with the Indians. He admired the Indians for their ability to quickly learn new skills and the fact he never heard of any Indians rebelling against their leaders. He said they were better to Europeans than Europeans were to Indians. Indians always offered food. Europeans looked upon Indians with scorn and disdain and thought Indians little better than beasts in human form. Yet Lawson maintained Europeans possessed more "Moral Deformities and Evils" than these "savages." But, even in his praise of Indians, Lawson referred to them as "savages".[46]

45   Marks, Geoffrey & Beatty, William K. *The Story of Medicine in America* p. 36 /39
46   Lawson, John *Voyage* p. 243/244

The Reverend Samuel Thomas was sent from England in 1702 by the Society for the Propagation of the Faith in Foreign Parts (SPG) to South Carolina. Thomas Nairne, later to become Indian agent, tried to interest Thomas in converting the Yemassee, and although Thomas did make some effort among the Indians, he decided not to continue working with the Indians. He wrote he had been told the Yemassee "had neither leisure nor disposition to attend Christian instructions." He was also afraid to be in Indian territory because of the war[47] then being fought. Thomas wrote, "… Their language is barbarous, savage and extremely difficult to attain, there being no grammar or rules for … learning." He added their language lacked any such terms as required to express Christianity. He asked a trader, who had mastered the Yemassee language, to translate the Lord's Prayer. Instead of "Our Father which art in heaven," the best the trader could do was "Our Father which art atop," and instead of "Thy kingdom come," it read, "The Great Town come." Thomas thought these were very improper. Thomas also pointed out the colonists also needed a minister and he took a dig at Nairne. He wrote that while Captain Nairne "who pretends to a great zeal for propagating Christianity among the Yemassee Indians, (he) has not evidenced the least Christian

47   The War of Spanish Succession, 1702 - 1713, called Queen Anne's War in English America.

concern for his ignorant slaves at home, of which he has many residing in his house, and so might be instructed with great ease."[48] Later Thomas served at St. James parish and Goose Creek where he died in October 1706.

Indians believed in two Spirits: the good one and the bad one. The good one they believed was the author and maker of everything who taught them to hunt and fish and made them wise enough to overcome the beasts of the wilderness. The bad spirit, who lives separately from the good one, torments with sickness, disappointments, losses, hunger and all misfortunes.[49]

Indian girls beginning at age 12 or 13 would sleep freely with male youths their age and that in no way stained their reputations. Marriage came later with consent from all parents and advice from the Indian king. Prior to the marriage being announced openly, the couple would often travel together for "several moons" to see if they liked each other. An adulteress was never put to death, but the wronged husband was given presents from his rival and the matter soon forgotten. On a few occasions a man would loan his wife out for a night or two.[50]

---

48   Kirk, Francis Marion *The Yemassee War* (Unpublished) p. 2 & 3 This should also be available at the South Carolina Historical Society in the SPG microfilm.
49   Lawson, John *Voyage* p. 220 & 221
50   Ibid. p. 40 & 41

And yet Thomas Nairne, during his westward expedition of 1708, reported the Chickasaw customs regarding women are "singulare" and much different from those of the other "savages." The Chickasaw women, among whom there was virtually no "whoreing," were not permitted "scandalous liberties" allowed the other Indian women. The young girls were carefully watched by their mothers and aunts least they should "make themselves cheap by being common." If an English trader should try and seduce a Chickasaw lady she would scornfully ask the trader if he thought she was among the Ochesses and not the Chickasaws. She would then add that the animals would mate for one night, but mankind needs to be more particular.[51]

The Indians were skillful hunters because game food was vital to their survival. Nairne reported the Chickasaws shot deer by setting a circular fire about four miles in circumference with the hunters posted as close as possible to the outside of the fire. When the deer tried to jump over the fire, the Indians would shoot them. Nairne did not mention what happened if the wind changed direction. In the spring and summer, the buffalo would eat great quantities of clay from clay pits where the Indians would kill them. The Indians would eat the bulls in May, June and July and the cows and heifers in the

---

51   *Nairne's 1708 Muskhogean Journal* p. 44/45

fall and winter. Many were shot because the buffalo tongue, which tasted like marrow, was a delicacy.[52]

A good time to hunt bear was from early January to mid March when they hibernated in holes. The Chickasaws would look in the holes under the roots of fallen trees or in hollow places in trees and when they found a bear nest they would fire it and shoot the bear as it ran out. After the bear was skinned, there was a layer of fat often weighing sixty to eighty pounds that was put in bags made from deerskins. It was important to have a good store of fat. The Chickasaw rule was that the one who found the bear received the skin and the belly fat.

Nairne was a great fan of the beaver and wrote he wished people had as much instinct for their own affairs as the "ingenious" beaver had.[53]

"Next to hunting and farming, the main occupation of most Indian males was the business of warfare. Like hunting, warfare was a passion ... To kill or capture the enemy filled his dreams almost as much as to slaughter and skin the deer or buffalo. For the most part, war was regarded as a solemn undertaking, not to be embarked on lightly. The days preceding the departure of the war-band were marked by a

---

52   Ibid. p. 52
53   Ibid. p. 54/55

mounting frenzy of rituals designed to bolster the morale of the participants."[54]

Indian cruelties to prisoners were legendary. They would inflict torments, such as scalping, that would prolong life as long as possible. The process was to cut off the skin from the temples and taking the whole head of hair along with it. Pitch pine[55] was split into splinters and stuck into the live prisoner's body. The splinters would be lighted and then the prisoner was made to dance around a great fire, with all the Indians deriding him until he expired. Then all would strive to obtain a bone from the unfortunate captive. This torture was called the *petite* feu. And it was the way John Lawson, Thomas Nairne and others were to die.[56]

In 1703 the King's lieutenant of Louisiana, Jean Baptiste Le Moyne sieur de Bienville, issued invitations to several tribes to lead war parties against the Alabama who had murdered three Canadians. "When Bienville and his sixty Canadians arrived at the rendezvous point, the war ritual had already begun ... the brisk autumn air was rent with war whoops and laughter as a procession of warriors danced through the grand square in the center of the Indian town ... Medicine men, covered with

---

54   White, Jon Manchip *Everyday Life of the North American Indians* p. 114 & 119
55   Pitch pine is a tree that produces resin, a substance that burns well.
56   Lawson, John *Voyage* p. 207

animal skins, burst from their magic-huts, shrieking in unknown tongues. Youths were flogged until their blood ran, the chiefs and old men exhorting them to bear their pain gracefully, as the warriors would do on the forthcoming expedition. The French and Canadians were so caught up in the spectacle, they joined in themselves, Bienville allowing his chest to be tattooed with figures of snakes, in the manner of the natives."[57]

North Carolina Indians were described as "a well-shap'd, clean made People." They were very straight and never stooped and had very well shaped limbs and their legs and feet "are generally the handsomest in the world." Their bodies were a little flat because they were laced to a board in infancy. Their eyes were black or a dark hazel and their bodies a tawny color. They rubbed their bodies with bear oil and burnt cork that made them seem darker. There were no facial hairs and they let their nails grow very long. Other than two families of the Machapunga Indians who used the "Jewish Custom" of circumcision, that practice was not followed by any other tribe. Shaking hands and scratching on the shoulder were the greatest displays of friendship. They never scolded children and were tender and indulgent to them. Many became addicted to liquor after its introduction by the Europeans. A few abstained, but most were not satisfied with just a little liquor,

57   Higginbotham, Jay *Old Mobile* p. 126

and they would drink until drunk. In these drunken binges they would sometimes murder or fall into the fire or break bones.[58] The English traders would dash their liquor with water but they charged the Indians as though it were not diluted. Indians also resold rum. During a Creek drinking bout one Indian woman, who had an empty bottle concealed in her mantle, would take long drinks from the bottle being passed around and then spit the rum into her concealed bottle until it was filled. Then the woman sold the bottle to a tribesman at her own price.[59]

"Indians initially believed that natural properties were transfused into humans through the food they ate. They believed those who ate venison ran faster than those who ate the slow-footed tame cattle or the heavy wallowing swine."[60]

Indians ate venison and most anything else including "Fawns in the bags, cut out of the Doe's Belly." Also bear, beaver, panther, raccoon, possum and squirrels roasted with their guts in, and all wild fruits. Young wasps, "when they are white in the combs and before they can fly," were a great treat. They ate all sorts of tortoise, shellfish and stingray as well as maize, wild potatoes, and acorns. They enjoyed beef, mutton and pork from the English. They ate fish of

58   Lawson, John *Voyage* p. 174/176/210/211
59   Axtell, James *The Indians' New South* p. 65/66
60   Ibid. p. 68

all sorts except the Lamprey-eel and the salt water Indians would not eat sturgeon.[61]

Indians also hired mourners for funerals. Their prostitutes, or "trading girls," who could perform abortions, were discernible by the cut of their hair. Their huts were often flea infested. Moss had many uses including tying poles together when building their cabins, diapers for children and personal hygiene for women.[62] Lawson also wrote, "The Indians are very revengeful, and never forget an Injury done, till they have received Satisfaction."

61   Lawson, John *Voyage* p. 182
62   Ibid. p. 189 & 197

THE WHITES

It is interesting to read about the Indian customs and tortures of the eighteenth century, but, in balance, we must compare the whites of that time to the Indians of that time and not compare twenty-first century whites to eighteenth century Indians. Some of the English punishments dictated by law could rival any torture the Indians had.

At the exact time the Carolina settlers were battling the "savages," the Jacobites[63] launched another in their series of rebellions in Britain. It was put down by December 1715 and the Jacobite prisoners were taken to London. "As two of the leaders of the rebellion arrived at Newgate prison, the corpses of three Jacobites were left in plain view before being placed on the gates as a warning to others." The prisoners, who had been drawn and quartered, had first been hanged, but cut down before they died

---

63   Oxford Dictionary "An adherent of James II of England after his abdication or of his son the Pretender; a partisan or supporter of the Stuarts after the Revolution of 1688." George I, monarch in 1715, considered Jacobites as traitors.

and then their bowels were taken out and burned before them after which their heads would have been severed from their bodies and then their bodies cut into quarters.[64] Often the headsman or hangman would slice open the chest, cut out the heart and say, "Behold the heart of a traitor."[65]

This punishment was reserved for traitors and Jacobites were considered traitors. Peers of the realm, who *were* convicted of treason, were usually simply beheaded at a public execution.[66] Drawing and quartering continued for other traitors until the reign of George III.

If a person, who had been arrested, would not enter a plea of guilty or not guilty in court, he or she was sentenced to be pressed to force him or her to make a plea. Any person who thought there might even be a remote chance of being found guilty would often not make any plea because the crown took the estate or any possessions of one found guilty. If one died from pressing, then that individual's estate could still be left to the family or to whomever the person had designated. Not until 1827 was an act passed directing courts to enter a not guilty plea when a prisoner refused to plea.[67]

64   Sinclair-Stevenson, Christopher *Inglorious Rebellion The Jacobite Risings of 1708, 1715 and 1719* p. 180 & 188

65   Andrews, William *Old Time Punishments* p. 202

66   Sinclair-Stevenson, Christopher *Inglorious Rebellion* p. 188

67   Andrews, William *Old Time Punishments* p. 203 - 210

A prisoner would be sentenced for pressing as follows: "That the prisoner shall be remanded to the place from which he came and be put in some low, dark room, that he shall lie without any litter or anything under him, and that one arm shall be drawn to one quarter of the room with a cord, and the other to another, and that his feet shall be used in the same manner, and that as many weights shall be laid on him as he can bear, and more. That he shall have three morsels of barley bread one day, and that he shall have the water the next day ..." Some prisoners would have 350 or 400 pounds placed upon them. As the practice of pressing was fading, prisoners who declined to make a plea were tortured by twisting and screwing their thumbs with a whipcord. In 1721 a Mary Andrews bore with fortitude the first three whipcords and submitted to plea on the fourth.[68]

Every English town had its public ducking stool used to duck "scolding women" in and out of a body of water which sometimes resulted in death. Along with the ducking stool were the public stocks, gallows and whipping posts. Vagabonds were the usual recipients of whippings, but sometimes the insane were flogged and even two people who had smallpox were flogged in 1711. The whip had three

---

68   Ibid. p. 203

cords knotted at the end. A 1791 statue expressly prohibited the flogging of female vagrants.[69]

Perhaps the most bizarre attempt at deterring crime was to hang the dead bodies of criminals in chains called a gibbet. If a person, for example, committed a horrible murder, his body might be placed in a gibbet and hung at the scene of the crime to deter other would be murderers. It was usual to saturate the body of the deceased criminal in tar so that it would last longer. A Lincolnshire murderer, Tom Otter, had his body placed in a gibbet in 1806 where it remained until 1850 when it was blown down. Some years later when the jaw bones became sufficiently bare to leave a cavity between them, a bird built its nest there. The discovery of nine young birds there gave rise to the following triplet:

"There were nine tongues within one head,
The tenth went out to seek some bread,
To feed the living in the dead."[70]

An example of a gibbet being used in South Carolina was reported in the *South Carolina Gazette* April 5 to 12, 1739. A slave, Caesar, who belonged to William Romsey was sentenced to be hanged for running away. The *Gazette* reported Caesar "was executed at the usual place, and afterwards was hanged in

69　　Ibid. p. 146
70　　Ibid. p. 230

chains at Hangman's Point opposite this town, in sight of all slaves passing by. Before he died he made a very sensible speech to encourage others to be just, honest and virtuous and to take warning by his unhappy example. After which he asked for those around him to pray for him as he repeated the Lord's Prayer."[71]

Although most of the cruel English punishments, such as drawing and quartering, were not used in South Carolina, many settlers in 1715 South Carolina had grown to adulthood in England and were well aware of the judicial punishments.

In 1703 in Charles Town's first major criminal case, Sarah Dickenson was sentenced to be burned to death. Sarah and her lover, Edward Beale, along with accomplice Joshua Brenan, were found guilty of successfully conspiring to murder their spouses. The men were hanged.[72] In England when a woman was burned, and it was usually women who were burned, she would be tied to a post with a rope around her neck so she could be strangled prior to the fire burning her. Sometimes they were not strangled.[73]

Hanging, which caused a slow, agonizing death, was the common capital punishment and prisoners were

---

71   Phillips, G.R. *Charleston's Past Post and Courier* April 4, 2002 p. 2ZB
72   Fraser, Walter J. *Charleston, Charleston* p. 22/23
73   Andrews, William *Old Time Punishments* p. 191

always hanged in public. Many people in Charles Town watched Stede Bonnet and the other pirates hanged in 1718.

Commissary Gideon Johnston,[74] rector of St. Philip's in Charles Town, wrote soon after his arrival in the early 1700s, "The people here, generally speaking, are the vilest race of men upon the earth. They have neither honesty, nor honor, nor religion enough to entitle them to any tolerable character, being a perfect medley or hotchpotch made up of bankrupt pirates, decayed libertines and enthusiasts of all sorts who have transported themselves hither from Bermudas, Jamaica, Barbadoes, Montserat, Antego (Antigua), Nevis, New England, Pennsylvania etc., and are the most factious and seditious people in the whole world …"[75]

Historian Edward McCrady took offense with what Johnston had written but did admit, "There were probably many characteristics of a newly formed community of bold, restless, adventurous men, who had thrown off the restraints and decorum of an old society, and had not yet formed another." McCrady maintained there were "many earnest Christian men in the colony."[76]

---

74 His title was commissary because he was the administrative assistant of the Bishop London.
75 McCrady, Edward *History of South Carolina* Vol. I p. 474
76 Ibid. p. 475

Charles Town was a robust frontier town with potential enemies on every side. Its streets were dirt but even worse it was not until 1704 a law was passed forbidding the slaughter of animals in city streets. Drunkenness was common and in 1703, 1709 and 1711 acts were passed to regulate the taverns and punch houses. Favorite alcoholic beverages included wine, cider, beer, brandy and rum punch. Often rum was mixed with water. The acts prohibited people from transporting liquor by boats or canoes for the purpose of selling it to the plantations because it was observed to be very "mischievous and to impoverish the otherwise sober planters" The act continued "... for each time *he, she or they* shall be convicted" the fine would be forty shillings.[77] Were there women selling liquor to the planters?

In 1705 a law was passed to prevent the stealing of horses and cattle. In 1712 Thomas Moore, "Gentleman of Berkley County," reported his house was broken into before daybreak and several pieces of silver plate were stolen. He did recover them.[78] Robbery was not unusual. Solomon Legare outsmarted robbers by keeping his valuables in plain view, but within an ordinary barrel that sat on his front porch.

---

77   McCord, David *Statues at Large of South Carolina* Vol. 2 p. 199
78   *Miscellaneous Records* Book 56 p. 87 Charleston County Library

The settlers, as well as the Indians, had a very high mortality rate. They suffered from smallpox as early as 1697 and distemper and yellow fever arrived in 1699. Yellow fever returned in "virulent form" in 1706 and 1711. Smallpox reappeared in 1712 and 1717 and a type of respiratory disease, probably the nature of influenza, killed many in 1707, 1711 and 1712. Infant mortality was exceptionally high.[79] There were doctors, but they could do little. Mosquitoes and gnats were a plague for much of the year.

There was greed, lawbreaking and immorality in South Carolina just as there is today, but there was also the great energy of pioneers trying to succeed. And along the way, good was accomplished. For example, a library and a free school were established early. Some would remember churches or ministers in their wills. Just as today, books were published on how to improve one's social graces and manners and these were to be found in South Carolina. Thomas Hepworth, Chief Justice of South Carolina 1724 – 1727, owned a copy of one of these self improvement books, *The Whole Duty of Man* published in 1660,[80] and it was listed in the inventory of his estate as being in an imperfect or a well used condition.[81]

79   Waring, Joseph I. M.D. *A History of Medicine in South Carolina 1670-1725* p. 18 /27
80   *The Whole Duty of Man* from Paul Goodman's *Essays in American Colonial History* p. 530
81   *Miscellaneous Records* Book 63 p. 83 Charleston County Library

THE GOVERNMENT ATTEMPTS TO REGULATE THE INDIAN TRADE

Perhaps Governor Nathaniel Johnson shared the view of others that Indians were revengeful and never forgot injury or insult until they received satisfaction. In Johnson's address at the opening of the second session of the Eighth Common Assembly on November 20, 1706, Johnson discussed several topics including Indians. He said the *"multitude of Indian traders were only concerned about profit and had no concern what the consequences would be in the future."*

The assembly began the process of regulating the Indian trade by taking the regulatory power from the assembly itself and giving it to a self-perpetuating board called the Commissioners of the Indian Trade.[82]

---

82 *Journals of the Commissioners of the Indian Trade* edited by W.L. McDowell, Jr. p. viii

After much back and forth among the assembly, the governor and council, "An Act for Regulating The Indian Trade And Making It Safe To The Publick" was ratified July 19, 1707. Its preamble stated, "WHEREAS the greater number of those persons that trade among the Indians in amity with this Government, do generally lead loose, vicious lives, to the scandal of the Christian religion, and do likewise oppress the people among whom they live, and their unjust and illegal actions, *which if not prevented may in time tend to the destruction of this Province...*"[83] The act required each trader to purchase an annual license for £8 unless the trade was only with the Lowcountry Indians including the Santees, Ittavans, Sewees, Stoanoes, Kiawahs, Kussos, Edistoes and St. Helenas. Thomas Nairne was named Indian agent with a salary of £250 per year and was required to spend at least ten months in Indian land. He swore not to take bribes, presents or fees from the Indians.[84] The original nine-members of the Board of Indian Commissioners consisted of Ralph Izard, James Cochran, Robert Fenwick, Colonel George Logan, Lewis Pasquereau, Richard Beresford, John Ash, John Abraham Motte and Major John Fenwick.[85] The main activity of the Indian commissioners was to curb the abuses of the traders and to obtain a small measure of justice for the Indians.

---

83   McCord Davis *Statues* Vol. II p. 309 (Italics added by author.)
84   Ibid. p. 309/316
85   Ibid. p. 315

The assembly even went so far as to also pass an act, ratified on July 19, 1707, to set the boundaries of Yemassee land. The boundaries were the Combahee River on the northeast, the marshes and islands on Coosaw and Port Royal Rivers on the southeast, the Savannah River on the southwest and to the northwest a line drawn from the head of the Combahee River to the head of the Savannah River and also one island called Coosawhachee. Whites were forbidden to settle in this area and those who had already settled would be paid to move. Settlers who refused to move would be fined £100.[86]

Regulations required no liquor be sold to the Indians, no ammunition could be sold to hostile Indians and if a trader should be convicted of selling any free Indian as a slave, the fine was £60. Also Indians could not be forced to give skins as presents to the traders. Each trader had to put up a £100 bond. This act was in effect until June 7, 1712, when another replaced it.[87]

The assembly began an investigation of traders accused of mistreating the Indians. After examining several people they found many complaints had been lodged against John Musgrove.

86   Ibid. p. 317/318
87   Ibid. p. 309/316

On December 11, 1707, the committee completed drawing up "Sundry Articles of Charge against John Musgrove" for abuses committed by him against neighboring and friendly Indians. Of the seven charges for which he was cited, most were for taking free Indians and selling them as slaves. Another charge against Musgrove included threatening the life of the Tuckesaw Indian king for not giving him four slaves and for stealing animals from Indians. The articles were read to Musgrove who generally denied them. Then he was ordered to withdraw from the assembly and a motion was made to put John Musgrove in the custody of Peter Mailhet, Messenger of the House, i.e. he would be placed in the watch house that was the jail. The motion did not pass.

The assembly then ordered Musgrove and the others not to leave the "Intrechments about Charles Town" and if they did they would be committed to the custody of the messenger. This order was shortly changed to have them remain within a thirty-mile radius of Charles Town. On December 20 the assembly "Resolved That it appears to this House that John Musgrove, John Pight, Anthony Probat and James Child are guilty of notorious Crimes Committed amongst the Indians" and ordered the attorney general, former Governor James Moore, to prosecute these men.

Also on July 19, 1707, the new Attorney General, George Evans,[88] was ordered by the assembly to present all papers relating to the misdemeanors committed by Musgrove, Pight, Probat and Child. Evans never presented these papers.[89] It would appear the only punishment was the temporary thirty-mile restriction.

David Crawley, a Virginia Indian trader, had his trading goods and some skins seized in 1707 by Carolinians because he did not have license to trade in the province. He wrote to Col. William Byrd in Virginia three and a half months after the outbreak of the Yemassee War his observations of South Carolina Indian traders. He said, "They would steal their hogs, fowl, corn, peas and watermelons." When the Indians came to their plantations to demand satisfaction, the traders would give a fraction of the value. If the Indians showed the slightest dissatisfaction, they would be cruelly beaten which they often were anyway according to Crawley. When goods like skins had to be carried in or out of Carolina, Indians were ordered to carry them and those who refused were beaten. Usually they were required to carry forty to fifty pounds and sometimes as much as 100 pounds any distance between 300 to 500 miles for

88   Evans was commissioned by the Lords Proprietors March 8, 1707, and apparently he was acting attorney general prior to his commission being registered by the Secretary of South Carolina on July 18, 1707.
89   Salley A.S. *Journal of the Common House of the Assembly June 5, 1707 – July 19, 1707* p. 71

very little pay. Former Indian agent, John Wright, had a great number of Indians to wait on him and carry the luggage and packs of skin from one Indian town to another "purely out of ostentation."[90]

Henri de Tonti, an early settler in lower Louisiana, wrote an interesting description of an Indian trader. In 1702 de Tonti led an expedition from Mobile to the Chickasaws. "Several of the natives greeted him warmly upon his arrival and conducted him to the entrance of the chief's cabin where a somber Englishman named Ajean faced them outside the door." Ajean may be a corruption of Johnson.

de Tonti described the first meeting, "They had us sit on piles of reeds facing the cabin. The chief was seated there along with an Englishman (Ajean) whom I had trouble recognizing as such. He was seated, holding a gun in his hands and a sword beside him. He had a very dirty blue shirt, no pants or stockings or shoes, a red blanket and necklaces around his throat like a savage. His main interest was in causing the destruction of Indian nations so he could obtain slaves."[91]

It took the Indian commissioners three years to disengage from the assembly. The separate entries of

90   BPRO Roll 2 Vol. 6 p. 100
91   Higginbotham, Jay *Old Mobile* p. 63/64

their journal began on September 20, 1710. In the opening pages of the journal, we find Musgrove and friends still up to their old tricks. The Indians complained to the Indian commissioners on September 21, 1710, that during the past spring Capt. Musgrove went to their town and demanded the Indians go and hoe his corn or he would beat them. The commissioners ordered Massony, an Indian of the Appalachias, be free until Capt. "Musgrave" could prove Massony was a slave. The same day the commissioners released Wansella, an Ellcombe Indian, from slavery until Mr. John Pight could prove him a slave.

And to top it off, Musgrove, served as one of the Indian commissioners from June 1712 to November 1714. However, John Musgrove was respected in the white community. And why would he not be respected? Practically every white person thought of Indians as barbaric savages so what difference did it make how they were treated. Some did realize that unless the Indians were treated properly, the province could be in great danger. Others, like Musgrove, apparently could not see that or were too greedy to care.

In 1711 and 1712 Musgrove represented Colleton County in the Thirteenth Assembly and he rose in the militia from captain to colonel by 1718.[92] At his

---

92   Edgar. Walter and Bailey N. Louise *Biographical Directory of the South Carolina House of Representatives* Vol. II p. 490

death, prior to February 8, 1724, he owned eight slaves, none of whom was designated as an Indian, 230 head of cattle and fourteen riding horses, all valued at £2,340.00.[93] His son, John, in 1731 did sell an Indian man named Justice to Daniel Green of Colleton County.[94]

John Musgrove, John Pight, Anthony Probat, and James Child were far from isolated cases. From the *Journals of the Indian Commissioners* we find, for example, on September 25, 1713, Lewis, King of the Pocotaligo Town, complained that Cornelius Meckarty and Samuel Hilden stripped and beat Wiggasay and Haclantoosa, two of his people, and took away their clothes. King Lewis also informed the commissioners that the Pocolabo king was coming with complaints against Dr. Ellis. The commissioners ordered the public receiver to arrest Edmund Ellis for trading without a license.

The next month the commissioners received information that Landgrave Thomas Smith had several traders working without licenses. The commissioners ordered they be prosecuted according to the law. On August 31, 1714, Charles Hart, president of the council, advised the commissioners he had revoked the license

93   *Wills, Inventories and Miscellaneous Records* Charleston County Vol. 58 p. 370

94   Ibid. Vol. 58 p. 317

of Indian agent, John Wright, for carrying rum to the Indians and had the attorney general, George Evans, arrest him. Hart told the commissioners the council expected them to provide proper evidence to prove the charges.

There were some who did trade legally with licenses. On October 14, 1710, Anthony Probat, James Lucas, Pight, and Probert, who in 1706 were charged with enslaving free Indians, posted the required bond to George Evans so they could take out their Indian trading licenses.[95]

On November 24, 1714, the Indian agent turned in the following trader's bonds permitting them to take out a license. Those included were: William Bannister, Thomas Barton, Jethro Bethridg, William B. Brett, Joseph Crossly, Joseph Cundy, Henry Evans, Richard Gower, John Graves, Edward Griffin, Roger Hoskins, John Jones, Cornelius LeMott, James Lucas, William Morgan, Charles Nicols, Charles Pierce, Anthony Probert, Roger Saunders, and Peter Scarlett. The sad fact is that of all these men only three, Bannister, Crossly and Hoskins, who had held licenses since 1710, had no complaints filed by Indians against them.

As late as 1711 the Lords Proprietors had been instructing Governor Charles Craven to take great

---

95   McDowell, William J. *Indian Journals* p. 4/5

care of the Indians and see they were not abused and that justice should be duly administered to them in South Carolina courts. Craven was further admonished to create a friendship with them to create better protection and stronger defense against the neighboring French and Spanish. It could have been written in 1690 as it sounded the same. Governor Craven later would find the last sentence of the instructions not to be true:"we assure you of our utmost assistance for your security."

But Indian complaints against South Carolina Indian traders never ceased. Some traders beat and killed Indians. Many stole from them, threatened them and worse.

The assembly and the Indian commissioners did make a serious effort to curb the abuses of the Indian trade, but they could never properly enforce the laws because Indian trading was big business and many people did not want the law enforced. Between 1699 and Christmas 1715, 708,215 half dressed deerskins were exported to the United Kingdom. The peak year was 1707 with 94,825 deerskins exported. This did not include undressed deerskins and sundry other animals such as otter, raccoon, beaver and one "leopard" in 1699.[96]

---

96   BPRO microfilm Roll 2 Vol. 6 p. 135/136

THE TUSCARORA INDIAN WAR IN NORTH CAROLINA & JOHN BARNWELL

After John Lawson's 1700 trek through South Carolina and North Carolina, he settled in North Carolina. He built a house about half a mile from the Indian town of Chatooka, the future site of New Bern. He was a surveyor and a naturalist. Lawson probably understood the Indians better and was more sympathetic to them than anyone else in North Carolina.[97]

Indian matters were no better in North Carolina than in South Carolina. As early as 1701, the Indians of the Pamlico River area complained to John Lawson that the settlers on Indian land "were very wicked people and that they threatened the Indians for hunting near their plantations." In 1703 the Coree Indians staged a minor uprising and were declared public enemies. An expedition

---

97   Lefler, Hugh Talmage *Introduction to a New Voyage to Carolina* by John Lawson p. xxxi

in 1706-1707 against the Mererrine Indians along the Virginia border seized thirty-six members of the tribe and imprisoned them for two days without food or drink. Their cabins were wrecked and the Indians were threatened that their crops would be destroyed if they did not surrender their land.[98]

Col. William Byrd of Virginia, writing about the traders of North Carolina said, "These petty rulers not only teach the "honester" savages all sorts of debauchery, but are unfair in all their dealings." Byrd declared the traders had abused the Indian women and mistreated the men. He said the Indians were weary of the tyranny and resolved to endure bondage no longer.[99] Were the Indian traders of Virginia any different than the traders of North and South Carolina?

The final action by the whites that led directly to the outbreak of the Tuscarora War was the settlement of New Bern in 1710 with the arrival of more than 400 new settlers. Within a few months of their arrival, there was serious cause for alarm among the Indians. The settlers took the best land along the Neuse and Trent rivers.[100] Lawson was a co-founder of New Bern.

---

98   Lefler, Hugh T. and Powell, William S. *Colonial North Carolina* p. 67
99   Ibid. p. 67
100 Ibid. p. 67

Under these dangerous circumstances, Lawson and a compatriot were captured by the Tuscarora because they thought the compatriot was the governor Edward Hyde. The Indians acquitted both of them, but Lawson got into a heated argument with an Indian king and was put to death by either having his throat slit or by the *petite feu*.[101]

Historian Edward McCrady said resentment and fear of punishment for murdering Lawson caused a general uprising among the Tuscarora. It began with a horrible massacre on September 22, 1711. One hundred and thirty white victims were butchered in the settlements on the Roanoke, sixty Swiss around New Bern were murdered and no one knew how many Huguenots were killed in Bath, North Carolina's oldest town. Women were laid upon the floors of their houses and great stakes were driven through their bodies. Pregnant ladies had their unborn children ripped from the womb and hung upon trees. The carnage lasted three days and terminated only as a result of fatigue and drunkenness.[102]

Governor Hyde immediately sent an appeal to Governor Alexander Spotswood of Virginia for help. One source states that Spotswood replied to the

101 Ibid. p. xix
102 McCrady, Edward *History of South Carolina* Vol. I p. 497/498

North Carolina request for troops by stating he could send troops only if North Carolina guaranteed provisions for them. North Carolina had limited funds and little food for its populations much less for an army. Therefore no help came from Virginia.[103]

Spotswood said no troops were sent because North Carolina would levy a 10% duty on all provisions that Virginia would carry into North Carolina.[104] Spotswood spent much energy defending his position not to send troops to North Carolina.

The reaction in South Carolina was quite different than was Virginia's reaction. Governor Robert Gibbes, the council and assembly immediately convened on October 26, 1711. It was at once resolved to help the North Carolinians. John Barnwell was made captain of the forces, an offer for which Barnwell thanked the assembly.[105]

Who was John Barnwell? He was the son of Matthew Barnwell and Margaret Carberry. He was born in Dublin circa 1672 and it was said he left Ireland "out of a humor to travel, and for no other reason." He was in South Carolina about 1701 and soon held

103   Lefler & Powell *Colonial North Carolina* p. 72

104   Original letters of Alexander Spotswood published in 1882 Vol. 1 p. 169 Virginia Historical Society.

105   McCrady, Edward *History of South Carolina Vol. 1 p. 498/499*

the office of deputy surveyor general. Barnwell, who was befriended by Nicholas Trott and Governor Nathaniel Johnson, was appointed clerk of the council in 1703 and promoted to deputy secretary in 1704. The same year Barnwell, an Anglican or churchman as they were called, opposed the Church Act because it discriminated against dissenters or non-Anglicans. Barnwell so strongly defended the rights of dissenters that he fell out of favor and was expelled from office. The Church Act of 1704, which was not approved by the Lords Proprietors, established the Anglican Church by law as the state religion supported at public expense and expelled all those who were not Anglicans from the assembly.

In 1703 Barnwell was ordered to map Port Royal Sound and he liked the area so much that in 1705 he obtained a 400-acre land grant on Port Royal Island. The original grant became "Doctor's," his resident plantation, but accounted for only a fraction of his landholdings that eventually totaled some 6,500 acres. All of his lands were located in the Beaufort - Port Royal area. Although he held many offices including that of representative in the assembly, it was as a frontiersman and Indian fighter that Barnwell made his name. After the Tuscarora War, Barnwell was known as "Tuscarora Jack." Barnwell and his wife, Anne Berners, had eight children, and there are many Barnwells in South Carolina today.

Colonel Barnwell's command consisted of a small number of militia and many more Indians. Captains Harford and Turston commanded 218 Cherokees. Seventy-nine Creeks were under Captain Hastings, forty-one Catawbas were under Captain John Cantey and, ironically, there were twenty-eight Yemassees under the command of Captain Pierce. They departed in mid November and after an arduous march through forests and swamps came upon the Tuscaroras January 28, 1712, in the upper part of the present Craven County, North Carolina. Barnwell's forces killed 300 and took 100 Indian prisoners. The survivors retreated into their fort in which the Indians had white prisoners. Barnwell, who was short on provisions, said he would withdraw providing twelve captives were released then, and the rest released by the end of the month. Also the Indians were to provide canoes for Barnwell's men to return to New Bern. A place and time were set to discuss the general peace. Barnwell's army reached New Bern on March 12. Many became ill there; several Indians died and Barnwell was so sick he could not keep the appointment to discuss peace. However, no Indians appeared for the conference.[106]

Barnwell raised more troops and early in April with 153 white men, including seventy North Carolinians, and 128 Indians they moved against the Indian stronghold. The siege continued for ten days, but was unsuccessful and all efforts to burn it failed. On April 17, pleading shortage of supplies, Barnwell ignored a directive from the assembly of North Carolina and signed a treaty of peace with the Tuscaroras. The treaty was very restrictive on the Indians and Barnwell, convinced he had completed his job, returned to New Bern. Marching back to South Carolina at the very end of June, he was seriously wounded in the legs, apparently by someone under his command. Since Barnwell was unable to mount a horse, he sent to Charles Town for a sloop to transport himself and his wounded men back.[107]

A rumor was circulated in North Carolina that Barnwell was miffed by that state's indifference to his actions in ending the war. The story accused Barnwell of breaking the peace by capturing some Tuscaroras and taking them as slaves in lieu of any payment North Carolina might have or should have given him. This rumor has been circulated in history as recently as 1972 in a thesis although Edward McCrady in his much earlier history stated it was not true. Lefler and Powell in their 1973 history, *Colonial North Carolina*, stated this was a "false charge." They continued, "An objective examination of the records shows that the Indians who were

---

107 Ibid. p. 77

to be sold into slavery actually were seized after Barnwell had boarded the sloop to return to Charles Town."

The Tuscarora resumed their attacks on the settlers in the summer and fall of 1712. North Carolina was again in a desperate plight made worse by yellow fever that took the life of Governor Hyde. Acting Governor Thomas Pollock immediately called on South Carolina again and in spite of North Carolina's ingratitude to Barnwell, Governor James Moore, with thirty-three whites and about 1,000 Indians, marched in November 1712 to the Neuse River. Cooperating with Pollock's forces they won a "glorious victory" at Fort Nohoroco on Contentnea Creek on New Year's Day, March 25, 1713. The victory dealt a fatal blow to the Tuscarora Indians of North Carolina. Because of the ruined condition of North Carolina, Pollock gave up any idea of completely wiping out the Tuscarora and instead turned to a treaty of peace. Moore remained in North Carolina attacking small bands of resistance, but by February 11, 1715, the bellicose Indians signed a treaty by which they agreed to live peacefully on a reservation near Lake Mattamuskeet.[108] Other Tuscarora fled north to New York to live with relatives among the Five Nations. All the Tuscarora finally left North Carolina by 1803.

---

108   Ibid. p. 79

THE FRENCH IN LOUISIANA, SOUTH CAROLINA'S MAIN COMPETITORS IN THE INDIAN TRADE

The French feared the English would bring about the downfall of the French colony along the St. Lawrence River. But they also feared the English in Charles Town would spread west to the Mississippi, cutting France's claimed territories, Louisiana and Canada, in half.[109]

For those reasons, the French royal court by 1697 felt an urgency to formulate a plan to colonize the lower Mississippi basin and the religious orders were beginning to become interested in this area for missionary work.[110] Pierre Le Moyne Iberville (1661–1706), navigator and North American explorer from a large Canadian family, was chosen to lead the naval expedition that got under way

109 Giraud, Marcel. *A History of French Louisiana* Vol. I p.3
110 Ibid. p. 11

October 24, 1698. Iberville was accompanied by his brother, Jean Baptiste Le Moyne sieur de Bienville (1680-1767). "As far as the minister of the French navy was concerned, the only purpose of the enterprise was to prevent the English occupation of the river's mouth and to begin an elementary reconnaissance." Only two ships were sent.[111]

The first colony was planted at Biloxi (now Mississippi) in 1699. In December 1701, Iberville decided the colony must immediately be moved to Mobile Bay. Mobile was laid out in March 1702 in a location further north than the site of the present city. Like Charles Town, the original site of Mobile had many problems so the town was moved to the present site in June 1711.[112]

Mobile was the only settlement in lower Louisiana until the founding of New Orleans in 1719. Until 1719, the words "Mobile" and "Louisiana" were interchangeable.

The initial number of colonists in Biloxi in 1699 was only eighty men, all of whom were in the pay of the king – soldiers, artisans, etc. For many reasons immigration was exceptionally slow and by 1708 there were only twenty-four families out of an

---

111   Ibid. p. 24
112   Ibid. p. 30, p. 186

overall population of 198.[113] Mobile was, at best, a muddy village with a small garrison.

French Protestants, called Huguenots, were included in the early population of Louisiana in spite of a policy to the contrary. "The official religion of Louisiana, Roman Catholicism, was believed to guarantee loyalty. It was considered dangerous to introduce into a colony very vulnerable to British aggression such persons whose Protestant beliefs might incline them to join with the enemy."[114] "Yet there were no doubts more than a few men of Protestant background were in Mobile during the colony's first decade of existence, just as there had been a significant number in Canada and in the French Antilles. Indeed, it would have been remarkable had there not been, considering the prevalence of Calvinism in La Rochelle and the surrounding towns of Saint- Martin (Ile-de-Re), Bordeaux and Saint – Jean d'Angely from whence the majority of Mobile's sailors, soldiers and craftsmen hailed. There were nine or ten residents at Mobile who had been baptized into the Reformed Church and numerous others whose families were of Calvinist background. These included Andre Penigault, Jacques Bernard *dit* Matagon, *matelot*[115] Rodolphe Direxen de Galambourg, goldsmith Louis Dore,

113   Ibid. p. 167
114   Marcel Giraud *A History of French Louisiana Vol. II* p. 35
115   sailor

habitant[116] Jean Bon and Canadian Jean Brunet *dit* Bourbonnois. Francois Lemay's mother, for example, was of Protestant parentage, and officer Jacques Barbazant de Pailloux's Calvinism was well known to the authorities."[117]

"Despite the existence of Protestants, little was made of their presence because none of those Protestants in Mobile had risen to a high station; they were not threatened because they were no threat themselves."[118]

The bad conditions at Mobile caused desertions by the French sailors, soldiers and artisans, all of whom were demoralized. Many sailors would jump ship at Spanish ports. Soldiers would find their way through the forests to South Carolina even though they feared being killed by the Indians loyal to England. But the English had begun in 1710 to forbid the Indians to kill them and the deserters were as warmly received in South Carolina as were the *coureurs des bois*.[119] "The English ban on persecution and torture of straying Frenchmen proved moderately successful once news of the policy became widely known and

---

116 A person who is to be billeted on the locals.

117 Higginbotham, Jay *Old Mobile* p. 380/381

118 Ibid. p. 381/382

119 Giraud, Marcel *A History of French Louisiana* Vol. I p. 221 – *coureurs des bois* were traders

believed."[120] Bienville wrote to Pontchartain[121] on June 15, 1715, that in 1714 seventeen soldiers had deserted to the English. He reported there were only forty soldiers at Fort Louis in two companies of whom ten were in no condition for service.[122]

One of these deserters married a South Carolina lady and they became traders among the Alabamas. The French called him not only a deserter, but also a traitor.[123] This Frenchman may well have been Francis Ryal mentioned in the *Journals of the Commissioners of the Indian Trade*. On November 18, 1713, Colonel Thomas Broughton advised the commissioners that one Francis Ryal, a French deserter from Mobile, was settled as a trader among the Alabamas. It was ordered that Ryall (the name is seen spelled as Ryal and Ryall) appear before the commissioners.

Francis Ryall, along with twenty-two other men, on November 24, 1714, took out a license to trade with the Indians.[124] Ryall then disappeared from any records.[125] It is not known if Ryall survived

---

120 Higginbotham, Jay *Old Mobile* p. 449
121 Jerome Phelypeaux de Maurepas, Count de Pontchartrain 1674 -1747. He was the Secretary of State of the French Navy 1699 - 1715.
122 Rowland, Dunbar & Sanders, Albert G. *Mississippi Provincial Archives 1704 – 1743* p. 183
123 Giraud, Marcel *A History of French Louisiana Vol. I* p. 318
124 McDowell, William L. Jr. *Journals of the Commissioners of the Indian Trade 1710 – 1718* p. 51, 58 & 63
125 Francis Ryall is neither mentioned in the *List of South Carolina Jurors, Land Warrants, South Carolina Chancery Court Records* nor *Wills & Misc. Records*.

the Yemassee War, but a George Ryall died in St. Helena's parish, South Carolina, in 1774.[126]

The *Journals of the Commissioners of the Indian Trade* mention only one other possible French deserter and he was not named either. On December 9, 1717, Captain William Hatton, principal factor appointed to reside among the Cherokees, advised the Indian commissioners that Governor Robert Johnson had been asked by a "French man" to send ransom to the Cherokees so they would release his daughter who they had taken. The commissioners approved sending the ransom so she could be returned to her parents who would repay the debt.[127]

As pathetic a colony as Mobile was, South Carolina feared Louisiana. The great fear was the French would win over the loyalty of those tribes allied with the English. Control of the Indians meant a lucrative trade and loyal tribes provided protection from enemies such as the French or Spanish.

Had it not been for one man, Bienville, the king's lieutenant, the Carolinians would not have had much to worry about. He was Louisiana's main asset in dealing with Indians. Bienville did not have the wherewithal to buy the Indian's loyalty as did

---

126 *Wills & Misc. Records* Book 95 p. 202
127 McDowell, William L. Jr. *Journals of the Commissioners of the Indian Trade 1710 – 1718* p. 239

the English so he had to rely on the resources of his personal ability at work. "His long experience with the Indians, his knowledge of their languages, the sincere friendship he showed them, and his generous hospitality enabled him to offset the gains of the British. Thanks to his personal qualities, he could reestablish in the most critical moments an equilibrium of forces, undoubtedly precarious, but sufficient to prevent the formation of the coalition sought by the British."[128]

When Canadian traders would arrive in Mobile with Indian slaves taken from tribes allied with France, Bienville would release them, especially if they came from weak tribes. He would execute Frenchmen for the unjustified killing of an Indian whose tribe was allied with France and he also punished Indians who killed Frenchmen.[129] "He even tried to gain the confidence of the tribes allied with England – and he did so without hesitating to engage in duplicity as he later confessed ... One of his methods consisted of returning to those tribes some slaves he had had his partisans capture, blaming the English for having initiated aggression in order to convince his enemies – by this pretended magnanimity – of his desire for peace."[130]

---

128 Giraud, Marcel *A History of French Louisiana* Vol. I p.206
129 Ibid. p. 207
130 Ibid. p. 208

Young Bienville could be tenacious as proven by his actions during a 1700 expedition, led by l'berville, to explore the Red River region. Twenty other Canadians traveled with them. They were advised not to attempt navigating the difficult Red River, but to go above it and go overland from the Tensas Indian village. They were greeted warmly by the Tensas, but during the night there was a large storm and lightening struck the Indians' temple that burned quickly. The medicine man called to the women to appease the Great Spirit by sacrificing their children. Five mothers responded by throwing their papooses into the burning fire. Afterwards the mothers were praised and caressed by the entire village.[131]

l'berville, because of a pain in his right knee, returned to Fort Maurepas leaving Bienville in command. It was March, winter was lingering and the countryside was being inundated by flood waters. Not only was every creek swollen into rushing streams, but much of the land was underwater in depths from knee high to over the head. Bienville, determined to show the Indians that the French were stronger and braver than the Spanish, pressed his group forward. They had to swim or wade naked across most of the icy cold creeks and rivers, pushing their clothes in front of them and firing off their guns to prevent

131   King, Grace & Ficklen, John R. History of Louisiana p. 51 Undocumented
Marcel Giraud in his History of Louisiana Vol. I p. 39 mentions the mission

possible alligator attacks. The Indian guides turned back saying they did not like walking and swimming naked all day in icy water, but Bienville pressed on covering ten or twelve miles a day, crossing six to twelve bayous and swamps. Often in the water, the men would be seized with chills and cramps and were forced to climb trees and stay in the branches until they recovered. To add to the discomfort, it rained constantly. Bienville later reported that he and his men never stopped singing and laughing to show the Indians they, unlike Spaniards, did not mind fatigue. What a sight that would have been to see - a tree full of cold, rain soaked naked men, singing and laughing while suffering from exposure. When they arrived at the Red River, they found most Indian villages inundated and abandoned, but the Indians Bienville found advised them to go no further. Because of their exhaustion, Bienville procured some pirogues and they paddled back.[132]

Bienville maintained the loyalty of the Choctaws, and periodically got the English leaning Chickasaws to sign a peace treaty giving the Choctaws a break from attack by the Chickasaws and in 1712 he brought the Alabamas back into the French fold.

---

132   Ibid. p. 54/55 Undocumented

THE WESTERN OFFENSIVE

South Carolinians realized that because of the French in Louisiana they had lost their near monopoly on the interior Indian trade they enjoyed prior to the 1699 settling of Louisiana. South Carolinians understood they could no longer be so casual in their trade policies and could not let abuses by unconscionable traders jeopardize their Indian alliances. As a result of this new understanding, Colonel Stephen Bull was sent in 1701 to the Alabama Indians to lay groundwork for an improved relationship with that nation by informing them of new directions in Anglican policy. The English regained the allegiance of the Alabamas and the Creeks of the Coosa and Talapoosa rivers.[133]

The beginning of the War of Spanish Succession in 1702 gave the Carolinians carte blanche to attack Florida and Louisiana and vice versa. This war gave impetus to the "western offensive." In 1702 South Carolina attacked and burned the town of

---

133 Higginbotham, Jay *Old Mobile* p. 123/124

St. Augustine, but had to withdraw because they could not capture the fort. In 1704 South Carolina attacked the Apalachees, Indian allies of the Spanish, who lived in the Florida panhandle. The Apalachees were murdered or forced to move toward South Carolina. In 1707 and 1712 Pensacola was attacked. In retaliation, in 1706 the Spanish and French unsuccessfully attacked South Carolina. Other plots were hatched as well.

In August 1705, John Musgrove, along with two other Carolina Indian agents, formulated a treaty that was finalized and declared all Indians allied with the French as "enemies to be attacked and annihilated" and the treaty affirmed the allegiance of all Creek tribes with England. "A grand council of the Indians convened at Caouita on the Chattahoochee River near present day Phenix City, Alabama. The council confirmed the treaty. Three thousand of the English allied Indians launched an assault against the Choctaws, who having been warned, fled to the woods. The Creeks ravaged and burned the Choctaw's cabins and crops before making a hasty retreat. When the Indians allied with English withdrew, the Choctaw emerged from the woods and launched a heated counter-offensive that resulted in the destruction of several hundred of their enemy. That temporarily ended the threat to Mobile."[134] "At the same time

---

134   Higginbotham, Jay *Old Mobile* p. 217 - 220

the English persuaded the Chickasaws to resume their attacks against the Choctaws, the missionary Fr. Cosme informed Bienville that English agents had incited the Chickasaws to capture slaves among the Choctaws ... From that time on, slave raids increased and the tribes, which were included in the French alliance, suffered incessant attacks, which caused the weakest nations to move toward Mobile ... The particularly warlike Alabamas harassed Pensacola and they led the powerful Creek tribes against the Thomes and the Mobiles, while the Chickaswas and Creeks ravaged the crops and villages of the Choctaws."[135]

"In October 1707, a year after the unsuccessful invasion of South Carolina by the French, rumors that were probably untrue, reached Charles Town that the French at Mobile were planning to assemble an Indian army to attack Carolina overland. This rumor prompted Thomas Nairne and Thomas Welch to propose a plan to strike against Mobile by seducing the French Indian allies, notably the Choctaws. If the French Indians could not be won over to the English, they were to be exterminated by an Indian army led by Nairne. The assembly approved the plan in November 1707, commissioned Nairne and Welch to undertake a diplomatic mission to the French Indians and, if

135 Giraud, Marcel *A History of French Louisiana* Vol. I p. 203/204

necessary, to conduct a war of extermination. His 'Journalls,' a record of that expedition, were filled with ethnographical data and acute observations that were of secondary importance to Nairne's group. The 'Journalls' were primarily the record of a secret diplomatic mission."[136]

"Nairne and Welch departed Charles Town at the beginning of 1708 ... and returned in May or June reporting success."[137]

Bienville offered a different viewpoint. He wrote in 1708 that "during the past spring two Englishmen (Nairne and Welch) arrived at the village of the Chickasaws to ask them to deliver presents to all the French allies. Nairne "went to the grand village of the Choctaw and was not very well received although he gave them a great present. The proposal that Nairne made to them in his speech stunned them: it was to aid them to destroy all the small nations that were nearest to Fort Louis at Mobile. Those nations included the Tomeh, Apalachee, Mobile, Tawasa, Chato, Pascagoula and Pensacola. The Choctaw refused to come to terms with Nairne who then immediately returned to Carolina."[138]

"Welch went to the Yazoo's village where he spoke to a congregation of Tensa, Natchez, Tunica, Arkansas

136 Nairne's *Muskhogean Journals* p. 15
137 Ibid.
138 Higginbotham, Jay *Old Mobile* p. 357/358

and Koroa. Offering peace to the assembled nations, Welch vigorously invoked their co-operation. The French at Mobile, he claimed, were in reality only refugees from France who the mother country would no longer support. This was the reason for the dearth of presents the French had to offer. The natives of the lower Mississippi villages made no reply to the harangues of Welch."[139]

According to Bienville's records, Nairne's expedition was a failure.

"When Bienville received news of English activity in the interior villages that summer of 1708 he was certain there was no immediate danger of attack," but he believed an attack would eventually come. Bienville used the threat of an attack to make the citizens of Mobile strengthen Fort Louis.[140]

In 1709 Bienville wrote to Pontchartain that the English of Carolina were sparing nothing to have the Indians that were allied with the French destroyed by those allied with the English. He complained that they came constantly in large bands "which accomplish almost nothing." He stated the Indians of the English came in canoes down the Alabama River in May with a force of 600 to 700 to destroy the Mobile and Tohomes Indians who lived only five

139   Ibid. p. 358
140   Ibid. p. 358

leagues from Mobile. The attacked Indians asked Bienville for help and he immediately went to them with sixty Frenchmen causing the Indians of the English to flee into the woods abandoning their canoes. Bienville had them pursued by his Indians who killed thirty-four and captured five alive who they burned in their village.[141]

The Choctaws, the most populous nation, was the only large tribe to remain with the French.[142]

Again in August 1709 Bienville wrote to France about another threat from the English. He reported that an Irishman who had recently fled from South Carolina brought word of a large invasion planned for that October. The expedition would consist of forty Englishmen, 2,500 Indians and three cannons.[143] As the Carolinians would plead during the Yemassee War for England to send troops, so did Bienville plead to France upon hearing this threat. He wrote that he only had seventy soldiers of whom one-fourth were children. He only asked for an additional twenty-five soldiers but added all the soldiers were destitute and needed clothes.[144]

141 Rowland, Dunbar & Sanders A.G. *Mississippi Provincial Archives 1704 –1743* Vol. III p. 136
142 Girard, Marcel *A History of French Louisiana* Vol. I p. 206
143 Rowland, Dunbar & Sanders, A.G. *Mississippi Provincial Records 1704 –1743* Vol. III p. 136
144 Ibid. p. 137

It was not that the Indians disliked the French, but that English trading goods were better and cheaper. Father Jacques Gravier wrote in 1706 that the Indians "naturally love the French," and he was convinced that if the French could have offered the same trading goods as the British had, the Indians would all ally with the French.[145] The French trading goods were never the same high quality as those goods the English could produce. French prices were always higher than English prices. Often those Indians who had strayed from English allegiance did not stay with the French for long. Father Gravier's opinion may have been biased but one historian wrote, "Yet on balance the French treatment of the Indian tribes seems have been more humane (than that of the English)."[146] In 1749 English trader George Croghan stated that no people carried on the Indian trade in such a fair manner as the French.[147] Perhaps the most realistic comment on the subject: "Although French traders were not angelic contrasts to their English counterparts – there were too many uninhibited Canadian traders in the colony for that – they did have the sense to realize that alienating their few allies and customers … was poor business and poorer diplomacy. So they learned the tribal languages … learned the patient protocol of the

145   Ibid. p. 210
146   Leckie, Robert *The Wars of America* p. 7
147   Axtell, James *The Indians' New South* p. 47

calumet (peace pipe) ceremony which often lasted three days and adapted themselves to the natives' strong preference for a fixed price schedule."[148]

Relations between South Carolina and Louisiana stabilized somewhat at the end of the War of Spanish Succession.

---

148   Ibid. p. 52/53

THOMAS NAIRNE

Nairne, a Scotsman, was in South Carolina by 1695 when he witnessed the will of Richard Quintyne, a Berkeley County planter. Richard Quintyne's wife was Elizabeth Edward, born in Scotland in 1658. After Quintyne's death his widow, Elizabeth, married Nairne. They had one son, Thomas, born in 1698 and died in 1718. Elizabeth, by her first husband, Richard, had three children.[149] Nairne's wife, Elizabeth, is buried at old St. Andrew's Church near Charleston, South Carolina.

"Nairne in truth was a soldier all his life. He commanded Indian and white soldiers during the unsuccessful South Carolina 1702 siege of St. Augustine and again in 1704 in raids against the Apalachee Indians who lived in Florida. Even his 1702 slave raid into Florida was a military venture as well as an economic venture ... As a member of the assembly he was often involved in military affairs. His plantation on St. Helena's Island was

149 Nairne's *Muskhogean Journal* p. 7

fortified and mounted with cannon to serve as the southernmost link in a chain of plantation forts along the seacoast. He also helped to organize a lookout and scout boat system to provide warning of Indian and Spanish raids along the frontier."[150]

Prior to this, Nairne had accused Thomas Broughton, son-in-law of Governor Johnson, of enslaving friendly Cherokees and of stealing 1,000 deerskins that belonged to the public. Johnson retaliated by accusing Nairne, among other things, of being a Jacobite and therefore being guilty of high treason. On June 23, 1708, Johnson threw Nairne into jail. Bail was not allowed in cases of high treason. Nairne was in jail for five months.

While in jail, Nairne wrote a letter to the Earl of Sunderland on July 10, 1708, that contained glowing plans for conquering the west. Verner W. Crane, the foremost historian of the southern colonial frontier, described the letter as "one of the most remarkable documents in the history of Anglo-American imperialism."[151] Nairne was writing in anticipation of the end of the War of Spanish Succession. Nairne, who could not know that war would continue for four more years, thought the war would end soon. Nairne wanted to make certain that the "English American Empire" would not be "unreasonably

150   Ibid. p. 9
151   Ibid. p. 3

crampt up" by the peace treaty. With the letter he sent a map he had drawn showing the locations of the Indians allied with the English and those with the French.[152]

It is indicative of Nairne's strong personality that he used the term the "English American Empire." Nairne quite clearly could see the empire stretching from Charles Town to Vera Cruz and Campeche, Mexico.

Nairne even had a plan to achieve the goal of this empire. Nairne proposed to fall upon the French with a force of eighty canoes manned by 500 Indians plus 1,100 more by land with fifteen English soldiers with the canoe party and thirty English soldiers with the land force. He intended to either destroy or remove into "our territory all the savages from Mobile to the Mississippi and up the river to 36 degrees of latitude." His plans did not stop at the Mississippi River as he wanted to capture the mines in Mexico that produced such great wealth for the Spanish. His plan included arming the Indians near the Bay of Campeche and then sending settlers "to exercise the trade of cutting logwood from that port," and also sending youths to learn Spanish, which must be done secretly, and when the time

---

152 BPRO Roll I Vol. 5 p. 193 /202

came these youths and settlers could oppose the
Spanish.[153]

Another paragraph from Nairne's letter gives
insight into the views of colonial whites towards
the Indians. "Our Indian friends the Talopoosies and
Chicasas employ themselves in making slaves of such
Indians about the lower parts of the Mississippi as
are now subject to the French." The good prices
the English traders gave them for slaves encouraged
them to ply the slave trade. Nairne wrote that
some men thought the Indian slave trade reduced
the number of enemy Indians the French could arm
and that it was a "more effective way of civilizing
and instructing then (by) all the efforts used by the
French missionaries."[154]

Nairne made it quite clear the trade between upper
and lower Louisiana must be ended. He proposed
enticing the Indians of the lower Mississippi to move
from French territory to English territory leaving
the lower Mississippi "desolate." Then the English
would set up trading posts on the Cussate River
(the Tennessee) and divert the trade from upper
Louisiana that formerly went down the Mississippi
River to the Tennessee and from there into South
Carolina. He reminded the Earl of Sunderland that
it was the English cloth, traded at the lowest price,

---

153 Ibid.
154 Ibid.

that kept the Indians loyal and urged duties should be kept a low as possible.[155]

Nairne's plan was not implemented because of the threat of the French and Spanish invading South Carolina. While still in jail, Nairne was reelected to the assembly and was finally released, however, the assembly, controlled by Johnson's men, would not permit Nairne to take his seat and they "called upon Johnson to issue a writ of election to replace him." Then Nairne "ran afoul of the Commons House over the conduct of his Indian affairs." He refused to turn over his map he had drawn of the southeast, and was again thrown in jail. "Nairne posted bond to obtain his release and sometime between December 1708 and April 1709 he 'absconded' to England to plead his case before the Lords Proprietors. In London, Nairne exculpated himself from the treason charge and was appointed by the Lords Proprietors to be a vice admiralty judge of Carolina." He was not reinstated as Indian agent at this time. Johnson was removed as governor because of his acts of high-handedness.

While Nairne was in England he wrote an article called "A Letter from Carolina in 1710" describing the events which had taken place.[156]

---

155 Ibid.
156 Nairne's *Muskhogean Journals* p.18

Nairne returned to South Carolina and was reelected to the assembly where he served in 1711 and 1712. He resigned when he was reappointed the province's Indian agent on December 18, 1712. He did not fight in the 1712 Tuscarora War.[157]

---

157 Ibid. p. 19

PRYCE HUGHES

Pryce Hughes, a Welshman, arrived in South Carolina in 1713 with a preconceived, grandiose plan to start a colony for 500 Welshmen on the Mississippi River, 120 miles from the French settlement.[158] "Thanks to Hughes, Britain was able between 1713 and 1715 to launch the most powerful offensive she had yet attempted to oust France from the Mississippi basin."[159]

Once again, this was a plan that would place a British colony on the Mississippi River to disrupt, if not eliminate, the French trading between upper and lower Louisiana. The French would do anything to see that this British colony was not established.[160]

Hughes left Charles Town in 1714 on an expedition to "site" his colony. By the end of 1714 Hughes had destroyed the system of Indian alliances that

---

158   Barker, Eirlys M. SCHS *Magazine* Vol. 95 p. 304/305
159   Giraud, Marcel *A History of French Louisiana* Vol. I p. 325 & Barker, Eirlys M SCHS *Magazine* Vol. 95 p. 325
160   Giraud, Marcel *A History of French Louisiana.* Vol. I p. 186

Bienville had established with the French. The French complained to South Carolina's Governor Craven and uttered threats of reprisals that were bluffs. The French decided to remove Hughes.[161]

In 1715 the French captured Hughes and he was taken to their fort at Mobile. He refuted France's claim to the area and informed Bienville that Queen Anne of Britain was about to send 500 families to Louisiana. Bienville treated Hughes well.[162] Bienville released Hughes because the governor of Louisiana had ordered that any captured Englishmen should be sent back.[163] Hughes was killed near Pensacola, Florida, as he was returning to Charles Town. No one actually knows who murdered Hughes.

---

161 Ibid. p. 326 & p. 328
162 Rowland, Albert and Sanders, A.G. *Mississippi Provincial Archives* Vol. 3 p. 182
163 Ibid. p. 187

GRANVILLE COUNTY PRIOR TO THE BEGINING OF THE WAR

Granville County, the fourth county established in South Carolina, extended from the Combahee (the "o" is pronounced as a "u" and the "a" is silent) River south to the Savannah River and from the Atlantic Ocean to an unspecified line far inland. Prior to the opening of the war, the Yemassees, who since their arrival in South Carolina had been faithful allies of the British, were living in five towns in Granville County: Pocotaligo; Huspa; Tomotley; Euhaw; and probably either Salkehetchie or Sapello. There were five other towns in Georgia. As stated, the Yemassee population in 1714 was 1,125 including 413 men, 345 women, 234 boys and 223 girls.

It is difficult to imagine today, but in 1700 the white population in South Carolina was a small minority in a vast land estimated to be between 5,000 and 6,000[164] and by 1720 had risen to only 6,400.[165]

---

164 Hewatt, Alexander *History of South Carolina* 1836 Carroll Edition Vol. I p. 132
165 Whitney, Edson *Government of the Colony of South Carolina* p. 116

The number of slaves was probably twice that. In 1715 the total number of Indians was 26,700 in the twenty tribes east of the Mississippi River that owed their allegiance to South Carolina.[166] There were also many Indians in allegiance with the Spanish and French, who posed another threat to South Carolina.

More than eighty-five white individuals had received grants to land in Granville County by February 25, 1715. Some of the earlier settlers had probably died by 1715, but more than likely their land was either sold to another family or passed on to family members. Two governors, Colonel James Moore, Senior, and Robert Daniell, who did not live in Granville County, were among the recipients of land.[167] Assuming there was an average of four members in each family and that would bring the total of white planter families to approximately 340 people. It was probably more than that.

Even though Beaufort had been granted a charter by the Lords Proprietors on January 17, 1711, and its two principal streets, Craven and Carteret, had been laid out, the "town" was virtually non existent in 1715. John Barnwell and Thomas Nairne are considered the founders of Beaufort. Although

---

166 Wallace, D.D. *South Carolina A Short History* p. 87
167 Consolidated Index Roll 7 p. 13777 & Salley, A.S. *Warrants for Lands*

there were no colonial towns in the county, there were assorted white people, other than planters, living there. For example, the Rev. William Guy had been sent to South Carolina from England in 1712 by the Society for the Propagation of the Gospel in Foreign Parts (SPG). Guy arrived in St. Helena's parish shortly before the outbreak of the Yemassee war. John Jordine had set up a punch house to illegally sell rum to the Indians at Capt. John Cochran's Point by 1714. Captain Cochran's plantation was located at modern Seabrook Point across the Whale Branch River from Yemassee land. White Indian traders were always wandering in and out and some of them, such as a John Fraser, lived among the Indians. Some traders had Indian wives or concubines.

By 1711, at least nine settlers had ignored the boundaries of the Yemassee land. They were William Bray, Joseph Bryan, Barnaby Bull, Isaac de France, Peter Hanes, Thomas Jones, John Palmer, Robert Steale and John Whitehead.

Apparently, some land grants had been improperly issued in the Yemassee land to settlers. Regardless, the white settlers did let their cattle graze on Yemassee land.

In 1715 raising cattle was becoming a big business. Some Carolinians owned 1,000 cows and owning

200 was very common. The Carolinians would produce salt beef for the West Indies in exchange for slaves, sugar and cash. The money was used to purchase land to raise a cash crop such as rice and many planters combined rice growing with cattle ranching. The cattle roamed freely in the woods. A herd of 200 cattle would require 3,000 acres of land and wherever cattle grazed the number of deer decreased. When someone like Joseph Bryan let his cattle roam on Indian land, the Indians found it increasingly difficult to meet their trade debts. Thus raising cattle in Yemassee lands was one of the contributing reasons leading to the Yemassee War.[168] Ironically "before the end of the century most southeastern tribes raised or rustled cattle themselves to compensate for diminished deer herds on diminished tribal Lands."[169]

In 1711 the assembly had ordered a sixteen-foot wide road to be laid out from the Ashepoo River to the islands of Port Royal and St. Helena's, but the road had not been completed by 1714. It was ordered, as it was with all roads, that the local inhabitants, their servants and slaves, aged sixteen to sixty, were responsible for building and maintaining the roads. The road to be built to the Port Royal area was to be overseen by the local road commissioners:

---

168   Otto, John S. *The Origins of Cattle-Raising in Colonial South Carolina 1670-1715 SC Historical Society Magazine Vol. 87 p. 117*
169   Axtell, James *The Indians' New South* p.68

Colonel John Barnwell, Captain Thomas Nairne, Henry Quintyne, Thomas Townsend and Captain Edmund Bellinger,[170] at least two of whom would not survive the Yemassee War. Townsend and Bellinger lived in Colleton County.

To enter Granville County by land, one took the road down from Charles Town crossing the Edisto and the Ashepoo rivers and continued to the causeway (or "causie" as they were called) that led across the Combahee swamp to the Combahee River ferry. The charge to cross was one half a rial for a man and one rial[171] for a man and horse, but ferries were free on Sundays when attending "divine service," and during times of militia muster or alarm.[172] Joseph Bryan was appointed "the keeper of the ferry."[173]

In 1702 the members of the Common House of the Assembly accused Joseph Bryan of abusing Indians. He was charged with stealing an Indian's canoe, killing the hogs and burning the house of another, and not paying the Indian who rowed his canoe.[174] Even worse, the assembly accused Bryan and some others, who lived in the southern part of the province, of possible disloyalty. Bryan was

170   McCord, David J. *Statues* Vol. IX p. 14 and 33/34
171   In 1707 a Spanish ryal was worth 7 pence ½ penny. In early South Carolina only foreign (non-English) coins were available.
172   McCord, David *Statues* Vol. IX p. 14 & p. 33/34
173   Ibid. Vol. IX p. 37
174   Salley, A.S. *Journals of the Commons House of the Assembly* 1702 p. 19

thought to be a "papist" and it was feared he would advise the Spanish in St. Augustine about Governor James Moore's forthcoming military expedition there. Bryan posted a £100 bond and the matter was dropped.[175] There is no mention of the "others" having to post a bond.

Bryan received a land grant for 550 acres in Granville County in 1705.[176] Then in 1711 he was one of the nine ordered to be prosecuted for encroaching on Indian land. In addition to perhaps living on Yemassee land, he let his cattle roam on the forbidden land. His son, Hugh, who would be captured by the Indians during the Yemassee War, would also operate a ferry in Granville County. Hugh and his brothers became wealthy.

Rumors of war with the Yemassees subsided a bit. April was the planting season and small farmers were in the fields with their family or perhaps one or two slaves. Planters like John Barnwell, with a larger number of slaves, were overseeing the operation of their plantations. The Reverend Mr. William Guy would be preparing for his Easter service. There was no church building so Guy rotated the services among the homes of the parishioners. Guy wrote to the SPG shortly after his arrival there saying that there were few who professed themselves of the

175   Ibid. p. 82
176   Consolidated Index Roll 7 p. 13778

Church of England. He thought this was caused by the long absence of a minister there.

Of the more than eighty-five individuals granted land in Granville Country prior to February 25, 1715, at least nine were licensed to trade with the Indians. It is probable that none of these Indian traders had totally pure records. Only three of the nine, Richard Hacher, James Pattison and Matthew Smallwood, had never had charges filed against them by Indians. Richard Beresford, president of the Indian commissioners, praised Granville County Indian trader, Evan Lewis. He said it was very good that Lewis had turned himself in and paid his Indian creditors. Beresford advised the commissioners to "give Encouragement to any Persons who shall see their Errors and repent of their Follies as Lewis has done." Colonel Alexander Mckay (or Mackay) had only one complaint lodged against him prior to 1715. An Indian king sent seven slaves from North Carolina with Colonel Mckay to be left at John Stanyarn's, but the king had no further word about the slaves.

Of the nine Granville County Indian traders, the ones who generated the most complaints were Cochran, Hilden and Daniel Callahan. Callahan had been causing complaints from Indians as early as at least 1702. In that year, the assembly ordered

Callahan to give satisfaction to the Huspah chief for two guns he had forcibly taken from an Indian widow.[177]

In 1711 John Cochran was prosecuted for selling a free Indian. Witnesses against Cochran were William Maggett and William Bray. Bray, who was already in trouble for encroaching on Indian land, turned right around and joined Cochran and others in accusing Samuel Hilden, a Granville County landowner since 1709, of purchasing Indian slaves illegally. Cochran and Bray were joined by Wenoya, an Indian, who complained Hilden had forced him to sell one of his slaves to Hilden for goods in the value of 160 skins. Hilden lost his license to trade with the Indians and then later was cited for trading with the Indians without a license.

The Indians filed many other complaints against these men and others.

---

177   Salley, A.S. *Journals of the Common House of the Assembly 1702* p. 21

WARNINGS AND THE LAST MEETING OF THE INDIAN COMMISSIONERS

Three warnings were given to South Carolinians concerning the impending Yemassee war.

A Yemassee named Sanute warned Hugh Fraser. It was common for the Indian traders, who resided among the Indians, to single out a particular influential warrior and to "court his favor" with presents and "constant civility." It is possible that Fraser was "courting" Sanute and that is why Sanute went to Fraser's house. Sanute brought Mrs. Fraser some sweet herbs to show his respect as was the custom of the Indians. After entering Fraser's house, he asked for a basin of water in which he bruised the herbs and used the mixture to wash Mrs. Fraser's face and hands. Then clapping his hands upon his own breast he told her in the future he would tell her all that was in his heart. Mrs. Fraser thanked him and gave him a present. Sanute returned about nine days prior to the opening of the hostilities and told Mrs. Fraser a war would soon begin. Because Mrs. Fraser was terrified, Mr. Fraser put his wife and child and his most valuable possessions into his boat and they fled to Charles Town. "Mr. Fraser, probably either discrediting what he had heard or from the hurry and confusion which the alarm occasioned, unfortunately had not taken the time to communicate the intelligence he had received to his friends who remained in a state of false security in the midst of their enemies."[178]

On April 12, 1715, the Indian commissioners met. Those present were Charles Hart, president, and Ralph Izard, Samuel Eveleigh, Richard Berrisford, Arthur Middleton and Henry Wigington. At this meeting the second and third warnings were reported.

First, William Bray reported to the Indian commissioners that while he was in St. Augustine looking for some of his slaves, a Yemassee Indian came to his wife, because of his great love for her and her two sisters. The Indian told Mrs. Bray the Creek Indians had a plan to pounce on the traders and then attack the settlements. He said the time of the attacks was near but he would come again to

---

178   Hewatt, Alexander *History* 1836 Carroll Edition Vol. I p. 193

let them know when they must leave and then they must leave immediately and go "to their town."

Assistant Professor William L. Ramsey has an interesting theory about the Bray family: that Mrs. Bray and her two sisters were Indians. Ramsey speculates, "It is difficult … to imagine in a colony with such a radically skewed sex ratio, that three English sisters would have lived together at a Yemassee Indian trading post." The Indian did not necessarily warn them because he was friendly toward her or even whites and he may have even waited until after Mr. Bray had gone to St. Augustine. "If, however, Mrs. Bray and her sisters were Yemassee Indians, then the Indian's 'great love' for them becomes a good deal clearer. The Yemassees, like other southeastern Indians, practiced a matrilineal system of descent reckoning, in which a warrior's first order of obligation was not to his own wife or children, but to his sister and her offspring." He suggests that "her town" may have been one of the Yemassee Indian villages such as Euhaw.[179]

The Commons House of Assembly on August 12, 1715, would give a commendation to the Indian Cuffy, who was from the Yemassee town of Euhaw, for bringing the first intelligence of the Yemassee Indians plan to massacre the English. He was given

---

179   Ramsey, William L. *SCHS Magazine* Vol. 103 January 2002 p. 62

£10 and a coat.[180] Larry Ivers and Francis Marion Kirk each wrote that the Indian who warned Mrs. Bray was named Cuffy and he was a Euhaw Indian.

The third warning came from Samuel Warner who advised the commissioners the Palachocola Indians had told him the Creek Indians were dissatisfied with the traders among them, particularly John Jones[181] and they had made several complaints without redress.

The commissioners ordered Warner to proceed on the governor's order to the Yemassee and Palachocola towns and then to the Creek. Warner was to ask the Indians to send some of their headmen to meet at Savano Town, located near present Augusta, Georgia, with the governor so he could hear their grievances. It was too little too late.

As the famous clock on the *Titanic* stopped at 11:30 pm on April 12, 1912, the entries in the Journals of the Commissioners of the Indian Trade ceased with the meeting of April 12, 1715.

---

180   Ibid. p. 60
181   John Jones survived the opening fury of the war and was ordered by the Indian Commissioners on January 28, 1717, to come down to Charles Town to answer complaints.

OUTBREAK OF THE YEMASSEE WAR

While the war is called the Yemassee Indian War, virtually all the Indian tribes in the southeast and mid south joined together to attempt to eradicate the white man from South Carolina. The assembly would estimate at least fifteen tribes were involved.

The general consensus is the war started because of trade abuses and harsh treatment of the Indians by the white traders, the debt the Indians owed to the traders and the fact that settlers were encroaching on their land. That is true, but the Spanish in Florida made it possible for the Indians to attack. More on the Spanish follows.

No one knows the exact date the war started. Many people say it started on Good Friday or Easter but that cannot be proved. An account in the Boston News on June 13, 1715, gives the date as April 16. Another account stated it was the end of April. Historian Alexander Hewatt says it was April 13. Perhaps the only really reliable date was that given by Francis Yonge as "that certain Day, in the Year 1715."[182] We do know the last meeting of the Indian Commissioners was on Tuesday, April 12 and the war started soon after that.[183]

Even though there had been a lull in war rumors, the Indian traders themselves must have been very nervous and anxious about the situation. Samuel Warner, as ordered, immediately went to the Yemassee town of Pocotaligo. Bray accompanied him.[184] Warner and Bray were joined in Pocotaligo by Nairne, Wright and possibly other Indian traders. "Nairne learned of the plan while at his plantation on St. Helena Island and hastened to Pocotaligo on his own."[185] Captain Seymour Burrows, captain of a scout boat, probably sailed some of the group over in his whaleboat. This group, which was going to negotiate with the Indians, with the possible exception of Nairne, was made up of the men the Indians hated the most. It would seem that if any chance of peace still existed, a worse group of people could not have been chosen to negotiate. The Indians gave no indication of their plans. They

---

182   Hewatt, Alexander *History* 1836 Carroll Edition Carroll Vol. 2 p. 145
183   According to *A Guide to the Commons House Journal of the South Carolina General Assembly 1692- 1721* Edited by Charles E Lee & Ruth S. Green (Commonly called Green's Journals) p. 393 The Assembly met on Saturday, May 7, 1715. Counting backwards, if I did it correctly, April 15 was on a Friday and could have been Good Friday.
184   Letter of George Rodd May 8, 1715. BPRO Roll 2 Vol. 6 p. 74
185   *Nairne's 1708 Journal* p. 20

were friendly, fed the traders and all went to bed seemingly happy that night.

The traders were awakened by the war whoop of the Indians who were painted red, the sign of war, and black, representing death. Only two or three people escaped, including a young boy, probably the son of a trader, who ran into the marsh. After nine days of hiding and starving, the boy wandered into the newly erected fort at John Woodward's plantation near the head of the Ashepoo River, about twenty miles from Pocotaligo.

Some of traders were shot, but others were tortured to death. Maccarty was apparently killed as his wife was taken prisoner to St. Augustine. Attorney General George Rodd wrote of his good friend John Wright being burned over a low fire and Thomas Ruffly was also tortured.[186] It was customary for the Indian women to apply the tortures.

Thomas Nairne suffered the "petit feu" torture. It was several days before he died.[187] On April 13, 1708, Nairne sent a letter from the Chickasaw lands to Robert Fenwick, a member of the board of the Commissioners of the Indian Trade. Nairne wrote, "It's now that season of the year, when nature

---

186   Ruffly's name is mentioned in the account of the war printed in the *Boston News* June 13, 1715
187   Letter of George Rodd BPRO Roll 2 Vol. 6 p. 74

adorns the Earth with a livery of verdant green, and there is some pleasure in an Evening ride up and down the savannas. When among a tuft of Oaks on a riseing knowll, in the midst of a Large grassy plain, I revolve a thousand things about the primitive life of men and think how finely on such a small Hill the tents might stand and from thence men have the agreeable sight of the Flocks feeding round them. Thus lived and rambled the great Patriarch in the plains of the East, thus stood the tents under and about the Oakes of Mamre.[188] In this state of life it was that the bright inhabitants of the Regions above designed to descent and converse with men."[189] You have to wonder if Nairne remembered his writing about that spring seven years earlier as he was suffering his agonizing death in 1715.

Hewatt reported that John Cochran, his wife and four children, the Brays and their two children and six more men and women, having found some friends among the Indians, were spared for some days. But they attempted to escape, were recaptured and all put to death. Beresford's prophesy about Cochran regretting the sale of a free Indian had come true.

George Rodd was in the Indian trading business and he had outfitted a man named Richard to go trade

---

188   Genesis 13:18 "Abram was living near the great trees of Mamre the Amorite, a brother of Eshcol and Anue, all of whom lived with Abram."
189   *Nairne's 1708 Journal* p. 58/59

among the Indians. Rodd wrote in 1715, "Another trader who escaped by the force of his horse said he saw Richard fall. I was told that he was not roasted and burned over a small fire. I did all I could to postpone his trip or make him take another route. I could have sold the merchandise for £300 sterling and I wanted to provide him an establishment in the colony, but he persisted strongly with his resolution (To go into Indian territory). I gave him two horses and I fitted him out and he promised to return near the end of the year. But the poor boy has been killed and all the merchandise lost. I am deeply touched by this loss. Because (of) other misfortunes I have no one at present to help me. I will never finish (this letter). Sir, if I told you in detail the deplorable state we are in ..."[190]

Traders, their wives, or Indian women with whom they lived, were all put to death in all the Indian towns on that first day of the war. One trader, while hiding, watched his fellow traders and their families being tortured to death.[191]

Seymour Burrows, a true hero of South Carolina, saved the day for hundreds of settlers. He miraculously escaped from Pocataligo although he was wounded twice. One bullet went in his neck

---

190   Letter of George Rodd May 8, 1715, Rodd BPRO Roll 2 Vol. 6 p. 81/82
191   Ivers, Larry *The Yemassee War in the Beaufort and Port Royal Area* p. 12 Unpublished.

or cheek and exited his mouth taking some teeth with it. The other lodged in his lung. In spite of these wounds, Burrows swam at least a mile and ran nine or ten miles from there to John Barnwell's plantation on Port Royal Island. The settlers were quickly warned.[192] Larry Ivers wrote that the killings lasted all day and about 90 people were murdered. Alexander Hewatt wrote that "only a few families of planters on that island,[193] not having timely notice, fell into their barbarous hands, some of whom were murdered and others made prisoners of war."[194]

By afternoon, just before the Indians reached Port Royal Island, a large number of settlers and some slaves[195] quickly boarded a boat in the Beaufort River. The authorities had detained *The Bachelor's Adventure*[196] and its captain, Joseph Swaddle, because there was suspicion of illegal trading. The matter, fortunately, had not been sorted out and the ship was still there at the outbreak of the war. The Indians, not finding anyone in the houses, went to water's edge by the ship. The settlers and Indians traded fire during the night while the Indians continuously chanted war cries, and at dawn, the ship, filled with

---

192 Letter of George Rodd May 8 1715 BPRO Vol. 6 Roll 2 p. 76

193 Hewatt did not specify which island.

194 Hewatt, Alexander *History* 1836 Carroll Edition p. 195

195 George Rodd gave the number as 400. That may have been high.

196 The name of the ship was found at South Carolina Archives in *A Guide to the Commons House Journal of the South Carolina General Assembly 1692 – 1721* Charles E. Lee and Ruth S. Green August 2 – 27, 1715 p. 445. This book is commonly called *Green's Journal*.

terrified refugees, made its way to Charles Town. The next day, with everyone gone, the Indians killed the horses and cattle and pillaged all they found. They danced in a grotesque manner and let out great cries of joy as they shot at and then burned the houses. George Rodd wrote a very unusual comment about the Indians actions, "Such spectacle could give one pleasure if the results were not so tragic."[197]

Others like the Rev. William Guy fled in small boats. Fleeing, he lost his horse and all his possessions except his clothes and his books. He wrote of a harrowing journey with another white man and three slaves, but they also made it to Charles Town.[198]

And we know, anyone fleeing by land, a risky route at best, would not have been charged for crossing on the Combahee ferry - if it were operating.

197   George Rodd letter of May 8, 1715 Roll 2 Vol. 6 p. 76/77
198   SPG records SCHS letters of September 20, 1715 and January 27, 1716.
296 (958 70/3) South Carolina Historical Society

REFUGEES

Charles Town was quickly inundated with terrified refugees. "Every one who came in brought the governor different accounts of the number and strength of the savages, insomuch that even the inhabitants of Charles Town were doubtful of their safety, and entertained the most discouraging apprehensions of their inability to repel a force so great and formidable."[199]

Hundreds of refugees stayed in and near Charles Town well into the hot summer making conditions, which were not pleasant, even more difficult. "A serious outbreak of flux (dysentery) promptly affected the inhabitants. During this time a hospital of a sort was in operation and while there is no account of its size or activities, there is an account of its existence. It sounds as though the establishment was part hospital and part refuge for refugees who had no means. Governor Charles Craven wrote the assembly on August 18, 1715, that the hospital

---

199   Hewatt, Alexander *History* 1836 Carroll Edition Vol. I p. 196

was in need of money for repairs.[200] Six days later Capt. Henry Quintyne asked the assembly that people then in the hospital be given three months provisions of corn and beef and then be discharged to such places as the government would direct. He recommended that all those who were sick should be provided with necessary items and that free Indian women should be sent to the several garrisons for the duration of the war.[201]

The Reverend William Guy, who had just complained how few parishioners he had in St. Helena's parish, had 105 of his "parishioners" show up on the doorstep of his wife's Tradd Street house and asked to be put up. William and Rebecca fed and gave them shelter for three weeks. Guy certainly practiced what he preached. The Tradd Street house must have been large because it would be chosen as the site of the Stede Bonnet pirate trials three years later. The owner of the house in 1718 was Garrett Vanvelsin. But the house could not have been so large that the logistics of managing sleeping areas, perhaps under tents, sanitary conditions and feeding the "guests," would have taxed the talents of the most talented general. Commissary Gideon Johnston wrote to the SPG that Guy's wife, Rebecca Basden Guy, had helped out with her small fortune.[202] Rebecca was

---

200   *Green's Journal August 2 – 27, 1715* p. 440

201   Ibid. p. 448

202   SPG microfilm 296 (958 70/3) letter of January 27, 1716

the granddaughter of the famous Quaker, Mary Fisher Bayly Crosse, who was in Charles Town by the early 1680s.[203]

The Reverend Francis LeJau, minister at Goose Creek, was in Charles Town for five months. Even the hero of the first day of the war, Seymour Burrows, fled to Charles Town where he recouped from his wounds prior to rejoining the fight.[204]

The Reverend Tredwell Bull, minister at St. Paul's parish, was forced to stay in Charles Town nearly four months. He wrote most of the men of his parish were "in little forts," and most of the women were in or near Charles Town. Nearly a fifth of the parish's residences, including Bull's, had been destroyed.

St. Bartholomew's minister, Nathaniel Osborne, barely escaped to Charles Town where he died July 13, 1715. He left a widow and two children "now in England."[205] This would indicate some people even left the province even though it was forbidden. Further evidence of people leaving is in Reverend Thomas Hasell's letter of December 1715, when he wrote that the fear about the Indians was so great

203 SCHS *Magazine* Vol. 12 p. 106/107
204 Rodd, George BPRO Roll 2 Vol. 6 p. 76
205 Bull, William Tredwell SPG Microfilm (958 70/3) Vol. 3-5

it forced the inhabitants to retire into Charles Town or "from thence to ship themselves off to other places."[206] George Rodd wrote that the only two ways to leave the province were with permission or to sneak out. Rodd begged for permission to leave if England did not send help. As is known, people did leave South Carolina for Virginia.[207]

About this same time, John Tate wrote describing the events that led to one man's desertion, a "piece of ill news" to an unknown recipient. He reported that Mr. Charleton who had purchased two boxes of tobacco, "ran away yesterday off the country" and owes you (the person to whom Tate wrote) £6 three shillings. Tate said he was sorry the recipient of the letter was the loser - making it clear it wasn't Tate's fault. Tate explained he tried to collect the money, but to no avail and (he) could not arrest him during martial law. To ease the pain, he wrote that Charleton owed a Mr. Jefferys about £200 and a Captain Devon of London about £300 more. Tate, who said he thought Charleton to be honest, ascribed the man's ruin to the war. Before the war all the traders, who owed Charleton a great deal of money, would stay at his house and now the traders have all been "knocked on the head" (killed by the Indians). Because the traders were all dead,

---

206   Hasell, Thomas SPG Microfilm 958 70/3 Vol. 3-5
207   Dodson, Leonidas *Spotswood* p. 35

Charleton has, Tate wrote, no way to collect his own debts.[208]

However, as late as December 1716, Boone and Beresford reported "the people (of South Carolina) are still decreasing by death and desertion."[209]

George Rodd in May 1715 wrote, "The people of the countryside come here from all parts; we hear constant cries and sobs from the women and the infants. Our misfortunes are great and they grow everyday by the famine; the deaths and sickness are worse than the Indians in such a way I despair of surviving so many ill things. We must not renounce all hope while we are alive."[210] However, Rodd had good reason for concerns about survival because he died in September 1716.

A few refugees also found their way to Mobile. Bienville wrote to Pontchartrian on September 1, 1715, about the Yemassee War even though he acknowledged Pontchartain had probably already heard the news. He stated, "This last summer all the Indian nations hitherto allied with the English murdered all the traders, who were among them, and that they even destroyed a part of the settlements of Carolina, burned their houses and killed their

---

208 BPRO Roll 2 Vol. 6 p. 124
209 Boone and Beresford Letter of December 5, 1716 BPRO Roll 2 Vol. 6 p. 269
210 Rodd, George BPRO Roll 2 Vol. 6 p. 85

livestock. At present they are all camped around Charles Town and are killing those who come out of it." Bienville continued that as soon as he heard he sent seven Frenchmen to the Alabamas, Talapoosa, Abihka, Kawita and several other nations close to Mobile to rescue any Englishmen not yet killed. Only one trader and one English woman remained alive and were taken to Mobile. The Indians told the French they had to kill the English because of the bad treatment they had received from them.[211]

No exact number of refugees who reached Mobile is given. Another source wrote, "Bienville even welcomed an English woman, possibly the same one mentioned above, the widow of a French deserter killed by the Indians, and he gave her the same rights as the salaried personnel to the privilege of the ration. The subjects who were received in the colony lived there peacefully while awaiting their repatriation ... the arrival of a British ship allowed the English men and women to return home."[212]

211   Rowland, Dunbar, & Sanders, A.G. *Mississippi Provincial Archives 1704 – 1743* p. 187 & 188
212   Giraud, Marcel *A History of French Louisiana Vol. I* p. 330

MILITARY RESPONSE

The governor at this time was Charles Craven, brother of William Craven who not only was one of the Lords Proprietors but was palatine. The palatine was the eldest of the Lords Proprietors. Governor Edward Tynte died in 1710 and his successor, Robert Gibbes was chosen in a bribed election. The Lords Proprietors were determined to make Craven, who was already in South Carolina serving as Secretary of the province, the governor. The proprietors so ordered it on February 21, 1711.[213] Gibbes did not resign immediately and Craven did not begin his service until March 19, 1712. Craven served until April 22, 1716, and it was during his term in 1712 the Lords Proprietors agreed South Carolina should formally adopt English common law as its own. Craven was reappointed governor in 1736, but did not serve. He died in England in 1754. Historian Edward McCrady called Craven the wisest and best governor of the proprietary era.[214]

---

213   BPRO Roll 2 Vol. 6 p. 137
214   McCrady, Edward *History of South Carolina Under the Proprietary Government* Vol. I p. 690

Governor Craven was en route to Pocataligo to meet with the emissaries and the Indians when he heard of the massacre. Craven had arrived at Captain Woodward's plantation.[215]

The Consolidated Index shows John Woodward (1681-1727) and his brother Richard (1683-1725), sons of Henry Woodward, owned land in Colleton County with land grants dating 1706 and 1705 respectively. Both were large landowners and both in the militia. The Directory of the Common Assembly indicates John was a captain circa 1710 and a colonel by 1725. Richard was a captain by 1725.

Craven took quick and decisive action. A cannon was fired from John Woodward's plantation to raise the alarm. The governor decreed martial law and he called up the Colleton County militia gathering a force of about 240 men.[216] Craven sent a dispatch by water ordering Lt. Colonel Alexander Mckay and Col. John Barnwell[217] to attack Pocataligo.[218] Where were Mckay and Barnwell? The Rev. William Guy in his letter to the SPG wrote, "... all the people fled from thence (St. Helena's parish) excepting

---

215 Rodd, George letter May 8, 1715. BPRO Roll 2 Vol. 6 p. 78
216 *Boston News* June 13, 1715
217 Rodd, George Letter of May 8, 1715. BPRO Roll 2 Vol. 6 p. 79
218 Kirk, Francis Marion *The Yemassee War*

about a dozen or fifteen men who remain in one fortification they have raised to watch the motions of the Indians by water."[219] Possibly two Indian fighters like Barnwell and Mckay were in that remaining fortification. Whether Mckay and Barnwell were in St. Helena's parish or Charles Town, they raised a force in excess of 140 men.

George Rodd wrote the Indians attacked the governor "even within the entrenchments" but they were soon repelled and "we took their *Sacs*[220] without any loss on our side."[221] Rodd is the only one who mentions this engagement and he did not state where it took place. He used "we" several times. Either he was a participant in this part of the campaign or he used the word "we" as "our side." Rodd continued that after the governor had taken the necessary measures and was advised his force was strong enough, he pursued the Indians. Craven and his troops advanced by land and the second or third night they camped on a plain near a river where there was a forest on each side.[222] According to the "Boston News," this site was sixteen miles from "Yamassee Town." The sentries said the Indians were in the forests split up "into several bodies."

219 Guy, William Letter of September 20, 1715 SCHS Microfilm 296/958 70/3
220 This French word, sacs, means sacks or sachels. Possibly they took the Indians sacks of provisions,
221 Rodd, George Letter of May 8, 1715 BPRO Roll 2 Vol. 6 p. 79
222 The river was probably the Combahee and the battle near Saltcatchers where the Indians had a large camp.

Rodd wrote, "we took all the precautions necessary and we were by our weapons all the night." The next day at dawn the Indians were ordered to fire "one shot of musket" that was the signal to attack. The Indians continued firing until one hour after sunrise and they had almost surrounded the camp having arranged them selves in the shape of a croissant.[223] At this point Craven rallied some of the runaway soldiers and the troops fell upon the Indians and put them on the run after having killed all their chiefs.[224] Thomas Nairne reported in his *Journal* of 1708 that when the Chickasaws were preparing a surprise attack on an enemy town, the warriors would place themselves in the shape of a half moon (or crescent) and march toward the village. When the chief warrior gave the signal with a whistle, each warrior would clap his hand to his mouth, give the war whoop and "then catch as catch can."[225]

A letter, oddly addressed to Craven, was found in the pocket of a dead chief, named Smith. The letter advised Craven to depart the country because all the Indians on the continent were united or would soon join them in this war. In conclusion, the letter said white men were old women in comparison with the Indians and several other insults of the same nature.[226]

---

223 Crescent shaped
224 Rodd, George Letter of May 8, 1715 BPRO Roll 2 Vol. 6 p. 80
225 Nairne's *Muskhogean Journal* p. 43
226 Rodd, George Letter of May 8, 1715 Roll 2 Vol. 6 p. 80

Craven did not pursue the enemy because of a lack
of guides, swamps and other tough terrain. His battle
had been won with only several men wounded and
one sentry killed.

The sentry, John Snow, was the first recorded soldier
to die in this war after the militia had been activated.
The Snow family was in South Carolina by 1699 when
Nathaniel Snow, Sr. received a grant for 300 acres and
another grant for 650 acres in 1704. Snow described
himself as a chirurgeon.[227] In 1703, the assembly voted
him £10 for his services as a surgeon with Governor
James Moore on the ill`fated attempt to capture
St. Augustine. Snow used his plantation home near
Goose Creek as a hospital and maintained a private
burying ground.[228] In Snow's 1728 will, he mentioned
his wife, Anne, daughter Sarah, and four sons, William,
Nathaniel (who married George Chicken's daughter,
Frances), Thomas and John. Since John Snow, the
sentry, died in 1715, obviously the John Snow in the
1728 will is not the same person. It cannot definitively
be said the sentry John Snow was the son of Dr.
Nathaniel Snow, Sr. although it was not uncommon
for parents to name a child after a sibling who had
previously died.

---

227 Archaic term for surgeon
228 Waring, Joseph I. MD *History of Medicine in South Carolina 1670-1825* p. 16

In the meantime, Barnwell and Mckay gathered their forces, at least 140 men, and sailed from Port Royal Island. They landed in Yemassee territory and marched to Pocataligo. The boats in use were small such as the popular ten-oared canoe that had a beam of about six feet and a length of about thirty-five feet.[229] Even if twenty men were crammed into each canoe, that would require a flotilla of a minimum of seven canoes. In other words, this was an early use in South Carolina of an amphibious landing.

Mckay was disappointed Craven was not at Pocataligo, but went ahead. After surprising the Indians, he attacked them and routed them out of the town. He then heard the Indians had moved to another fort where they were at least 200 warriors and Mckay sent about 140 men to attack that fort. At that time a youth named John Palmer, who had been scouting with about sixteen men, came to McKay's aid. They scaled the walls of the Indian fort, attacked the Indians in their trenches, killed several, but they were met with such fierce resistance they had to retreat outside the walls. The group re-entered the Indian fort and forced the Indians to flee into the arms of Mckay, waiting outside, who killed many of them.[230]

229   Ivers, Larry E. SCHS *Magazine* Vol. 73 p. 122
230   "Boston News" June 13, 1715

Mckay, one of the heroes of these battles, was in Granville County by 1706 when he received a land grant for 500 acres. His name was spelled McKay or Mackay although the Scottish clan spelling is MacKay. His name was spelled Mackay in the "Boston News" in 1715. He was elected to two assemblies, but declined to serve. Instead he devoted his time to the militia and was a captain by 1709 and was a major in 1711 during the Tuscarora War. He rose to lieutenant colonel by 1715 in the Yemassee War. Mckay died before April 11, 1723, leaving his widow, Helen, a small estate of £366 and five slaves.[231] The name McKay comes from the Gaelic MacAoidh that means son of fire,[232] seemingly a very appropriate name for an Indian fighter.

After these battles, the surviving Yemassees fled to Florida. Mrs. Sisson and Mrs. Macartey, who had been taken there by the Indians as prisoners, later reported that the Spanish in St. Augustine received the Indians with ringing bells and firing guns as though they had been victorious in the field.[233]

Mrs. Macartey was the widow of Cornelius "Meckarty," one of the Indians traders against

231 *Directory of the Members of the Common Assembly* Vol. II
232 MacDougall, Margaret O.& Barn, Robert *Clans & Tartans of Scotland* p. 189
233 Hewatt, Alexander 1836 Carroll Edition *History of South Carolina* Vol. I p. 198/199

whom the Indians had lodged complaints to the commissioners of the Indian affairs. Even so, imagine how Mrs. Macartey felt to see the people who murdered her husband being treated as heroes.

Hewatt wrote that when Craven returned to Charles Town "the people were raised from the lowest state of despondency to the highest pitch of joy. Craven entered Charles Town with some degree of triumph and receiving from all such applauses as his wise conduct and unexpected success justly merited." The "highest pitch of joy" was not to last as more difficult days were ahead.

In August the assembly would vote to pay for two "pipes"[234] of wine to be placed in Governor Craven's cellar. This was a present from "this House" for his great service to South Carolina. The assembly also voted to send one pipe of wine to Deputy Governor Col. Robert Daniell and also voted to postpone until the end of the war an investigation into charges he had been spending public money.[235]

---

234 A pipe is a cask.
235 Green's Journals p. 439

GOVERNMENTAL RESPONSE AND RELATIONS WITH OTHER COLONIES

Craven and council had declared martial law, laid an embargo on all ships and vessels "belonging to South Carolina" which were in any South Carolina harbor, pressed into service many of the inhabitants and slaves, seized many horses, arms and ammunition for military use and took several other necessary measures. Craven also made Robert Daniell deputy governor to act while Craven was away from Charles Town fighting Indians.

The Fourteenth Assembly[236], like Craven, wasted no time in doing what was necessary to ensure a favorable outcome to the war. The assembly met everyday from Friday, May 6 through Friday, May 13. There was even a meeting on a Sunday, the 8th of May. On that Sunday the members of the assembly wanted to adjourn the session so they could return

---

236 The Fourteenth Assembly met in nine sessions between September 22, 1713, and October 13, 1715.

home to build fortifications. The request was denied. The assemblymen, particularly those from the outlying areas, must have been frantic to get home to protect their families.

On Friday May 6, its members, including Speaker William Rhett, listened to an impassioned speech by Governor Craven in which he said the recent actions by the Indians were barbarous and that "We are still almost naked and defenseless."[237]

On Saturday May 7 the governor, the council, and the assembly made major decisions. Some of these included:

1. That a treaty be made with the Cherokee Indians
2. Provisions were to be secured for the distressed people
3. To collect what rice or other provisions that remained at any deserted plantation or other places
4. That Thomas Island, now Daniel Island, and James Island be appointed to receive refugees.
5. To take an inventory of the guns that were on board the several ships in the harbor.
6. The enemy Indians were to be destroyed. Black slaves were to be armed. Craven informed

237 *Green's Journal's* No. 4 p. 388 South Carolina Archives

London he had "enlisted 200 Negro slaves because of the shortage of white men in the province."

With an Indian enemy force numbering in the thousands and South Carolina able to muster at most about 1,500 men, all available men, including slaves, had to be used. The assembly voted to pay for arms for those Negroes whose owners could not supply them and a law was passed making it illegal for any slaves to be sent out of the province.[238]

The slaves performed so well South Carolinians would not use them again for fear of slave revolts and the Yemassee War was the only time white colonial South Carolinians used black slaves in combat.[239]

The same day, May 7, the assembly and council wanted Colonel James Moore, Jr., to be commissioned as commander with a sufficient force "to destroy the Indians." Moore was ordered to take, kill and destroy all Indians "not in amity" with the province's government.[240] This was not a policy of unconditional surrender, but a policy of absolutely destroying any Indian who was against the province.

---

238   Ibid. p. 391 & 392
239   Jabbs, Theodore *The South Carolina Colonial Militia 1663- 1733* p. 293
240   Green's Journals p. 395

South Carolina had always considered the primary threat of enemy attack to be by the French and Spanish and the primary route of invasion to be by sea. Thus the few defenses that existed were along the coast. Its land and sea forces were paid volunteers, few in number and spread out entirely along the coast with a small permanent force maintained in the fortifications of Charles Town. The militia had not fought Indians since the first decade of the settlement and its tactics were limited to the European mode of fighting. Indians served as soldiers alongside whites and sometimes outnumbered them. Before the outbreak of the Yemassee Indian War, South Carolina's Indian allies, the Yemassees, Cherokees, Upper Creek, Catawbas and Chickasaws, were relied upon to defend the southern and western approaches to the province. Abruptly the outbreak of the war made South Carolina's defense policy totally obsolete. South Carolinians scrambled. From then on South Carolina maintained a series of frontier garrisons.

The policy of building garrisons basically began on May 7, 1715, when the assembly urged garrisons be built on the following locations:
1. on the property of John Ball
2. on the property of Dr. Nathaniel Snow Sr. in Berkley County

3. on the property of Steven Wiatt - This garrison was to be used for the reception of women and children in distress.
4. on the property of Captain Benjamin Schenckingh which is now under Lake Marion
5. on the property of John Hearn which was about forty miles northwest of Charleston and the property is now on the western bank of Lake Marion
6. at Wassamassaw, the cowpen of Ralph Izard
7. at Edisto Bluff plantation
8. on the property of the late Richard Godfrey on the Ashley River in St. Andrew's parish
9. at the plantation of William Ford near Wando River
10. On John's Island possibly near James LaRoche's bridge

The first two were probably not built.[241] The next year the number of garrisons was scaled back.

An example of a garrison from the Yemassee Indian war can still be seen. In 1717 Thomas Hepworth, who lived in Charles Town, built a small house[242] in Beaufort. Gun slits were cut through the above ground phosphate basement walls to protect

241 Green's Journals p. 392
242 214 New Street

against an Indian attack. He built the house to meet a residency requirement so he could run for the assembly. It was easier to get elected there than Charles Town because, as we know, every white person in Granville County either had been murdered or fled to Charles Town. Hepworth represented St. Helena's parish for three terms.

Usually a garrison was a relatively small wooden stockade sometimes built around an existing house. They were usually manned by thirty to fifty militiamen and slaves. Those militiamen and black slaves not on garrison duty were divided into two provincial armies – one in the north and one in the south.

The *Bachelor's Adventure*, apparently, was still in Charles Town on May 7. On that date the assembly recommended using vessels smaller than Captain Swaddle's to be sent to "fetch provisions to the Southward."[243]

May 7 was a long day. The assemblymen asked that candles be brought in and their wish was obeyed.[244] It was probably about 7:30 pm when the candles were requested.

After the candles were lighted, the assembly agreed to invest the governor with all laws necessary to

---

243   Ibid. p. 393
244   Ibid. p. 396

carry on the war. They also read letters from Col. Barnwell and Capt. Fenwick stating how necessary it was that martial law should be invoked to keep the soldiers from deserting.

On May 10 Act 350 was ratified and it stated the actions that had been taken in the war by the governor, deputy governor and members of council were "hereby" confirmed. Any lawsuits that may have arisen from necessary actions were to be discharged and declared void. The same day Act 351, "An Act to Impower the Right Honourable Charles Craven, Esq. Governor, and His Council to Carry on and Prosecute the War against our Indian Enemies and their Confederates," was ratified and three commissioners, John Bee, Captain John Cock and Edward Bradford, who were exempt from military duty except under the most drastic circumstances, were appointed. They were to carry out the orders of the governor and his council. These orders could include impressing ships, arms, ammunition, provisions, etc. They were to appraise all seized goods and give the owners receipts so they could be reimbursed by the assembly. Martial law was not to extend beyond military affairs. Even the wounded and people who lost everything in the war were remembered. The commissioners were empowered to seize, for these needy people, medicines, spices, sugars, linens, and all other appropriate items from the citizens. The seized goods could also be used for various reasons to insure victory. The act was to remain in force for only three months.[245]

Also on Tuesday, May 10, Capt. Fenwick sent an express message to the assembly requesting that all officers in the assembly immediately return to their units. Their example on the field would keep soldiers from deserting.[246] How bad was the problem of desertion?

In a later session of the assembly on August 23, 1715, province treasurer, Alexander Parris, ordered the assembly to pay him a £100 present for his extraordinary services to the public.

The same day Rhett received permission to go to England from governor Craven to defend himself from charges brought against him by Capt. Joseph Swaddle.[247] The next day, August 24, Swaddle sent a petition to the assembly asking for £50 to repair damages to the *Bachelor's Adventure* made by the Indians. During that awful night at the opening of the war on the ship, that held so many horrified settlers, the Indians did damage the ship from firearms. There could have also been flaming arrows hitting the ship.

---

245   McCord, David *Statues* Vol. II p. 623-626
246   Ibid. p. 406
247   Ibid. p. 445

Swaddle was brought to the assembly and told by Rhett that his petition was false.[248] The charges may have been that Swaddle accused Rhett of trading illegally. But Swaddle probably was doing the same thing. And they possibly were trading illegally together. Swaddle and Rhett hated each other.

"Landing Chief" sculpted by Peter "Wolf" Toth
1977 – Charles Towne Landing, site of Charles Towne's original settlement.

248   Ibid. p. 447

Cassique of the Kiawah, Charles Towne Landing

A reproduction of the 1678, 34 ton ship *The Adventure* –
Charles Towne Landing.

St. Philip's Episcopal Church, est. 1680, Charleston, SC

Tombstone of Gov. Robert Daniel – St. Philip's. Inscription reads he died in 1718.

The Old Powder Magazine c. 1713 – Charleston, S.C.

Col. William Rhett's House c. 1712 – Charleston, S.C.

The Thomas Hepworth House 1717 – Beaufort, S.C. The house, built as a garrison during the Yemassee War, has gun slits in the raised basement.

St. Helena's Episcopal Church c. 1721 – Beaufort, S.C.

Edward Chisolm Jackson and Suzanne Motte Peronneau
Jackson – descendants of Henry Woodward, Mary Fisher
Bayly Crosse and Thomas Hepworth

EMISSARIES

Emissaries were sent abroad to ask for assistance. The "Impowering Act" of May 10, 1715, provided for the seizure of skins and other necessary items, not to exceed the value of £2,500, to be used to fund a ship to go north to purchase arms and ammunition.[249] A letter dated August 25, 1715, written to South Carolina's agents in England, Joseph Boone and Richard Berresford, which was signed by Robert Daniell, Arthur Middleton and Benjamin Godin, reported that council member Benjamin de la Conseilleire returned from Boston August, 18. It may have been de la Conseilleire who took Craven's report of the war to the "Boston News," which published it on June 13, 1715. de la Conseilleire returned with about 600 arms purchased with the seized goods. He reported the Massachusetts government and particularly the governor, Colonel Dudley[250] were so "ungenerous" that if de la Conseilleire had not taken the goods with him, he would have returned empty handed.

---

249   Ibid. p. 625
250   Joseph Dudley (1647-1720) An unpopular governor who served 1702-1715.

The letter continued stating the arms arrived in a timely manner to furnish the army then being raised.[251]

One source states emissaries were also sent to New York to purchase weapons and that Craven praised Robert Hunter, governor of New York and New Jersey, for seeking to rouse the Senecas to aid South Carolina.[252] The Senecas did not aid South Carolina and there is no record arms ever arrived from New York. However, Governor Hunter wrote Governor Spotswood in Virginia that the northern Indians had become very turbulent and ungovernable and evidently gave Spotswood to understand that no assistance would be coming from New York.[253]

One group of emissaries went to England itself. Mr. Kettleby,[254] agent in England for South Carolina, reported during a meeting of "His Majesty's Commissioners for Trade and Plantations" on July 16, 1715, that Mr. Johnson[255] and several Carolina planters, merchants and master of ships had "lately arrived." They must have departed Charles Town immediately after the outbreak of the war as it took

---

251   BPRO Roll 2 Vol. 6 p. 134

252   Wallace, D.D. _South Carolina A Short History_ p. 89

253   Dodson, Leonidas p. 33

254   He was the Honorable Landgrave Abel Kettleby and was still alive in 1722.

255   There were two Peter Johnsons in South Carolina in 1717.

three months to cross the Atlantic.[256] Did they take their families with them? The South Carolinians reported "to their Lordships" the extremities to which that province is now reduced because of the Indian war. The gentlemen advised that "for the most part" the citizens had been driven into Charles Town. When asked what caused the war, they replied the lack of "good government" among the Indian traders might have given provocation. They added the trading laws were not well regulated and in addition that the laws that were on the books were not observed. They asked the king to make South Carolina a royal colony and send 500 troops.[257] The royal government, not the Lords Proprietors, sent 1,000 muskets, 600 pistols, 2,000 grenades, 201 barrels of powder and one or two warships came from northern stations.[258] The *H.M.S. Shoreham* was one of those warships that called on Charles Town.

The Carolina delegation could not have arrived in England at a worse time to request aid. Britain was headed for another Jacobite Rebellion. "The accession of George I on August 1, 1714, had been engineered so smoothly that no one had an

256 It usually took two to three months to cross the Atlantic from Charles Town. For example, a letter written in Charles Town on August 6, 1716, was received in England four months later on December 5, 1716. BPRO Roll 2 Vol. 6 p. 235 It may have been shorter in spring or summer. A copy of each letter was usually sent on board a separate vessel.

257 BPRO Roll 2 Vol. 6 p. 140

258 Wallace, David D. *South Carolina A Short History* p. 89

opportunity to protest. A few hotheads in Devon had proclaimed James Stuart as king and there had been a Jacobite inspired riot in Bristol the previous October. The atmosphere remained comparatively calm until the Whig dominated parliament met in March 1715. From that moment, the more extreme Tories began to consider very seriously the Jacobite alternative ..."[259]

"Throughout May, tensions had been rising, and there was one particular violent outburst in Oxford, always a center of Stuart sympathies ... On June 10, James' birthday. There were great demonstrations in the north and west. The government took action, even if local governments were either too disloyal or too frightened to follow their example.[260] On July 15, the day prior to the meeting between the Carolina emissaries and Commissioners for Trade and Plantations, the Jacobite uprising was debated in the House of Commons. The Riot Act was renewed and the impeachments of Tory leaders were approved. But the disturbances continued to spread ..."[261] The British government was facing a fight for its own survival at the very time South Carolina, fighting for its own survival, arrived to ask for assistance. However, by October the rebellion in England had been put down, actually before it

259   Sinclair-Stevenson, Christopher *Inglorious Rebellion* p. 100
260   Ibid. p. 104
261   Ibid. p. 105

began, and the rebellion was crushed in Scotland by the end of the year. George I remained on the throne. Still it is amazing the Carolinians received any assistance at all from the British government.

VIRGINIA

Soon after the Yemassee War began, Arthur Middleton was sent to Virginia to negotiate with Governor Spotswood. A South Carolina act, the text of which is now lost, passed August 27, 1715, appointed agents to transact the affairs of the province with the governors of Virginia and Maryland[262] and to "Accommodate the Articles already made with the governor of Virginia"[263]

For sometime before the war, there had been animosity between Virginia and South Carolina. Virginia had had virtually free access to the southern Indian trade until South Carolina was settled in 1670. The South Carolina Indian act of 1707 clearly stated that "all and every person" trading with the Indians must pay the £8 license fee required to trade with Carolina Indians. It was then when goods of Virginia traders, such as David Crawley and Robert Hix, started to be confiscated and Virginia began to complain bitterly. In 1708 Virginia made charges to

262 John Hart served as Royal governor of Maryland 1714-1715 and again as governor 1715-1720 under the restored Proprietary Government.
263 McCord, David *Statues* Vol. 2 p. 626

the Lords Proprietors that skins of their traders had been illegally seized by South Carolina. The proprietors replied that South Carolina's Attorney General, George Evans, was due in England any day and they would investigate.[264]

In spite of Queen Anne ordering Virginia traders to be allowed to pass through Carolina freely, the Carolina assembly passed an act in 1711 that specifically required traders from Virginia and other provinces to come to Charles Town to take out a license.[265] This was very inconvenient for the traders. As late as March 26, 1715, Spotswood wrote to Craven protesting the license fee stating that Virginians were the first English subjects to establish a trade with the Indians to the southwest of the colony long before the existence of Carolina. He said the Virginia traders had been ruined by "the oppression and violence of the Carolina Traders and their Agents..." He said any citizen of any of his Majesty's plantations (colonies or provinces) still had a "free Liberty" of trading with any Indians within Virginia. He continued that no other colony or province had ever "pretended" to confine the Indian trade to its own inhabitants, "nor to lay such dutys as equivalent to a prohibition" (of the trade). Then he threatened that Virginia traders, if they chose, could under price South Carolina traders.

264   Ibid. Vol. 5 p. 212
265   McCord, David *Statues* Vol. 3 p. 357 Act 299

While they had no intention of doing that, the Virginia traders had much more money than they used to and would "spare no costs to prosecute their designs with vigour ..." Spotswood hoped both governments would strive to "improving a good Correspondence" between them and expected a reply with the return of the ship which took the letter to South Carolina.[266]

Spotswood entrusted the letter to Captain Meade of the *H.M.S. Success* that arrived in Charles Town just at the time of the outbreak of the war.[267]

Even with the confusion of the time, a short, albeit terse, reply was sent to Spotswood on June 22. All of Spotswood's issues were totally ignored. He was informed that Samuel Eveleigh, a member of council, had an affidavit from a young man who was very positive that the "Cuttabaws" had declared they received encouragement from the Virginia traders "which put them upon this action" (to revolt). The affidavit said some Virginia traders had stolen goods from an Indian trader named Titmarsh who was among the "Cuttabaws" when the war broke out. It was thought that Titmarsh had been killed.[268]

---

266   Edited by William P. Palmer MD *Calendar of State Papers (Virginia)* Vol. 1 p. 180/181

267   Cheves, Langdon City of Charleston *Yearbook* 1894 p. 320 n. 4 Cheves prepared the article for publication.

268   *Calendar of State Papers (Virginia)* Vol. 2 p. 181

Deputy Governor Robert Daniell in a letter of August 25, 1715, to South Carolina's agents in London complained about actions being taken by Virginia. Word had reached South Carolina that the northern Indians had met with Governor Spotswood to make a peace and arrange a trade agreement with Virginia. The treaty had not been concluded by August 25 because the Indians left to obtain approval from their chiefs. South Carolina wanted Virginia not to conclude any treaty with the Indians until the Indians "make Satisfaction" for the great damages they had incurred. It was the feeling of South Carolinians that Spotswood was attempting to monopolize the Indian trade under the pretense of making peace. Daniell also feared the Indians could inflict even more damage on the province unless the king of England ordered Virginia not to sell any more goods to the Indians.[269] The only influence South Carolinians might have over the Indians would be if they could control, at least temporarily, the goods, including rifles, which were sold to the Indians. If goods could be purchased elsewhere, such as from Virginia traders, South Carolina would virtually be at the mercy of the Indians.

Colonel George Chicken recorded in his journal on December 30, 1715, the Cherokees would not fight against the "norrode" (Virginia) Indians because

---

269 BPRO Roll 2 Vol. 6 p. 131

Governor Spotswood had given each Indian a gun and a blanket and promised to trade with them if they remained "still and quiet" and not fight the English.

In addition to the bitterness Virginia and South Carolina had for one another because of the license issue, there was also bitterness concerning the supplies and men Virginia sent to South Carolina to help put down the Indians.

How much the Virginians contributed to South Carolina's aid is a matter of whom you wish to believe. It is a fact that Spotswood sent express messages to his fellow governors of Maryland, Pennsylvania and New York urging them to defend their own borders[270] and to send aid to South Carolina. Spotswood sent copies of these letters to South Carolina.[271] These governors sent no aid. Samuel Eveleigh wrote in October 1715, the government of Maryland was "in arms." Maryland had been confronted with an alarm from the frontier counties that the Potomac Indians might go on the warpath, and its council sent to England for arms and ammunitions.[272] Spotswood is given some credit by the South Carolinians as being sympathetic to their plight. Upon receiving a plea from Craven,

270   Wallace, D.D. *South Carolina A Short History* p. 89
271   Rodd's letter of July 19, 1715 BPRO Roll 2 Vol. 6 p. 105
272   Dodson, Leonidas *Spotswood* p. 33

Spotswood and the Virginia council immediately sent 160 muskets, twenty-five casks of shot and ten barrels of powder that arrived in Charles Town just before mid July. Shortly afterwards, Middleton arrived from his mission to Virginia with 120 white men.[273] Rodd wrote in his letter of July 19, 1715, that Spotswood had been "very cordial" and had gone to a lot of trouble to send men to South Carolina. Spotswood's biographer, Leonidas Dodson, wrote, "Spotswood in his efforts to raise the men may have supported his promises with some sort of personal guarantee" This led to many debtors hounding Spotswood and he wrote that it pained him that he should be suspected of contriving to kidnap Virginians into the service of another province.[274] Thirty more Virginians did arrive later in July.[275]

Afterwards when Spotswood convened the Virginia House of Burgesses, its members were dissatisfied with what Spotswood had already done and they refused to send more men. These actions were attributed to the assembly's "ill Disposition" towards South Carolina.[276]

---

273   Letter of George Rodd July 19, 1715. BPRO Roll 2 Vol. 6 p. 104
274   Dodson, Leonidas *Spotswood* p. 36/37
275   Letter of George Rodd July 19, 1715. BPRO Roll 2 Vol. 6 p. 107
276   Letter from Boone and Beresford to the Commissioners of Trade & Plantation December 5, 1716. BPRO Roll 2 Vol. 6 p. 264

However, the conditions Spotswood put on his initial offer of aid had very high terms. Spotswood requested payment of thirty shillings per month per man and one female slave be sent to work in the place of each man sent to South Carolina.[277] Leonidas Dodson, wrote that the "acceptance of such hard terms seems to indicate either a very urgent need of assistance, or a lack of intention to carry out the bargain."[278] South Carolina did not honor Middleton's agreement and instead paid the men £4 each per month.[279] This was the same pay the Carolina soldiers received. No slaves were sent for fear it would cause a slave uprising. South Carolinians, at even this early date, realized slaves could be pushed only so far.

Virginia even sent an envoy, Francis Kennedy, in an endeavor to get South Carolina to live up to Middleton's agreement, but he failed. Kennedy was then sent by Virginia's council to represent them in England.[280] In October 1715, Colonel George Evans and Robert Fenwick were sent to Virginia for more aid, but Spotswood said it would be impossible to

---

277   Ibid. p. 262
278   Dodson, Leonidas *Spotswood* p. 35
279   Dodson, Leonidas (p. 36) wrote it was four pounds each for the eight or nine months. Boone and Beresford wrote it was four pounds per month. BPRO Roll 2 Vol. 6 p. 263
280   Dodson, Leonidas. p. 37

get more men to go since South Carolina did not live up to Middleton's agreement.[281]

What did the Virginia troops contribute? Spotswood, on one occasion, complained the Virginians, in violation of the agreement, had been scattered among the South Carolina militia. Contradicting himself on another occasion, he wrote the Virginians had repulsed an attack against Charles Town by 700 Indians while Craven was marching north in the opposite direction.[282] That is not true. As the troops were departing South Carolina in mid March 1716, Boone and Beresford wrote, South Carolina was willing to let them go because the province could not afford to keep them any longer.[283]

Spotswood and his council wrote a letter to England that resulted in a hot response from Boone and Beresford on December 5, 1716, to the Commissioners of Trade and Plantations. Virginia had claimed that because of the troops they sent to South Carolina, His Majesty had been spared sending his own troops as had been requested. Boone and Beresford related the whole saga and defended South Carolina's actions. They said that

281   Ibid. p. 35/36
282   Morton Richard L. *Colonial Virginia* Vol. II p. 438 Morton cites Spotswood p. 131/132
283   BPRO Roll 2 Vol. 6 p. 160

such a powerful neighbor as Virginia should have helped South Carolina at its own expense as South Carolina helped North Carolina in 1711. They wrote the demand for female slaves was unreasonable and told them of paying the soldiers more than had been asked to compensate for not sending slaves. They reported that South Carolina had paid for about 130 men, most of whom were "poor Ragged Fellows" who were raw servants transported to South Carolina immediately after their arrival in Virginia. Their masters only sent them because they would make more money with them going than staying. Many of the servants, who were "unseasoned" to South Carolina, fell ill. They were entirely "unserviceable" and inexperienced in military matters, nor were they in any action.[284]

So Virginia officials stated their soldiers were abused heroes and South Carolina officials said they were worthless as soldiers and did not participate in any action. As is often the case, the truth is somewhere in the middle. More follows on the Virginia soldiers.

---

284 Boone and Beresford letter of December 5, 1716 BPRO Roll 2 Vol. 6 p. 261 - 264

THE WAR CONTINUES

The war took a turn for the worse. A post on the Edisto River was abandoned by weak and fatigued militia when enemy Indians were spotted on the opposite shore. Down from the north, the Siouan, allies of the Yemassee, crossed the Santee in late May to pillage and burn. When the Indians reached John Hyrne's plantation, about fifty miles from Charles Town, they approached peaceably, and after Hyrne had given them provisions, they murdered him and everyone there.[285] John Hyrne and Jonathan Drake, jointly, are recorded as having a warrant for 500 acres of land in Berkley County in August 1709.[286] If this were the same place, Hyrne in six years of ownership, would have probably just gotten his place in order and have begun to harvest some crops.

Militia Captain Thomas Barker, "a brave young Gentleman ... who fought at the Battle of Combahee,"[287] gathered ninety horsemen, but was led into an ambush in a thicket by a treacherous

285 Hewatt, Alexander *History 1836 Carroll Edition* Vol. I p. 196
286 Salley, A.S. *Warrants for Land* Vol. III p. 218
287 Letter of August 20, 1715, by Tredwell Bull SPG microfilm 296 (958 70/3)

Indian. A large party of Indians lay concealed on the ground and Barker advanced into the middle of them before he was aware of the danger. The Indians sprang up and fired upon Barker and his men from every side. Barker and twenty-six of his men fell at the onset and the survivors were forced to retreat in confusion.[288] The treacherous Indian has been identified as a Wateree, who was once owned by former Governor James Moore, Barker's father-in-law, who had given the Indian his freedom.[289] Moore had died in 1706.

Once again a stream of refugees fled into already overcrowded Charles Town. The residents of St. Johns, St. Stephens and St. James parishes left their plantations behind. Goose Creek became the northern frontier of the province and only one small fort remained beyond that point. It was located on Captain Benjamin Schenckingh's cowpen on the south bank of the Santee River, twenty miles northwest of present Moncks Corner.[290]

Schenckingh's fort was garrisoned by seventy white men and forty blacks who resolved to remain and defend themselves in the best manner they could. They surrounded themselves with a breastwork.

288   Hewatt, Alexander 1836 Carroll Edition *History* Vol. 1 p. 196 and BPRO Roll 2 Vol. 6 p. 103
289   Hicks, Theresa M. (edited by) *South Carolina Indians and Indian Traders* p.42
290   Ivers, Larry *Colonial Forts of South Carolina* p. 73

The commander of the fort was named Redwood. A John Redwood is mentioned only twice in the Consolidated Index, both times in court cases in 1713. In one of the cases Dr. Nathaniel Snow filed suit against him.[291]

The Indians could not capture the garrison by force so they pretended to want to make peace. Redwood ordered his men to disarm and let the Indians into the fort. Upon gaining entrance, each Indian, at a given signal, drew a tomahawk concealed beneath his blanket and proceeded to massacre the unarmed garrison.[292]

A resident of Charles Town wrote on July 19, 1715, that Indians, upon entering Schenckingh's fort, used tomahawks and knives and "knocked" twenty-two of our men on the head, burnt and plundered the garrison. According to him, four white men were taken prisoner by the Indians but were rescued by George Chicken.[293]

Unfortunately, Redwood's legacy is his gullibility in believing the Indians, but he paid for his mistake with his life and the lives of most of his men.

291 Consolidated Index Roll 13 p. 25870
292 Kirk, Francis Marion *The Yemassee War* p. 10 Presented to the Society of Colonial, Wars in 1950.
293 A letter supposedly written by George Rodd to Joseph Boone and Richard Beresford, agents of the Province in London. *City of Charleston 1894 Yearbook* p. 319/320

Soon after, Captain George Chicken marched with 120 men from The Ponds located near the head of the Ashley River. In 1893 The Ponds was called Schutz's Lakes. They marched four miles to a plantation where the men were divided into three groups. Two groups were ordered to find and surround the Indians to prevent them from fleeing into the adjacent swamp, but before they could accomplish this, two enemy Indians, who were scouting, discovered Chicken and his men. Chicken killed the two Indians to prevent the rest from discovering them, and he immediately attacked the main body of the Indians. Chicken and his men killed about forty Indians.[294]

The four prisoners rescued by Chicken said the Indians had numbered about seventy and that they had taken Stephen Ford's son from the fort to their towns and nothing further had been heard. Stephen Ford was in South Carolina by January 6, 1700, when he received a warrant for 300 acres. By 1709 he had accumulated a total of at least 1,540 acres in Berkley and Colleton counties.

Chicken's campaign was concluded by June 6, 1715.[295] All was quiet until about July 24.[296] Because it was

294 George Rodd's letter of July 19, 1715. *City of Charleston 1894 Yearbook* p. 319/320

295 BPRO Roll 2 Vol. 6 p. 128 & p. 130 – The source of the date of June 6 is found (p. 130) in a letter dated August 25, 1715, written by Robert Daniell, Arthur Middleton and Benj. Godin. Francis Marion Kirk in *The Yemassee War* (Unpublished) also uses the date of June 6. Historians William J. Rivers, Langdon Cheves and Edward McCrady set the date as June 13.

296 Cheves, Langdon *City of Charleston Yearbook 1894* p. 322

quiet, Governor Craven gathered a force of about 700 and marched from The Ponds on July 18 to the plantation of Colonel Thomas Broughton near present Moncks Corner.[297] From there Craven's army headed north to meet Colonel Maurice Moore of Cape Fear, North Carolina. The plan was to meet and join forces on the north side of the Santee River at the Winyah River to make a strike against the northern Indians. Moore, the son of Carolina Governor James Moore who served 1700 to 1703, was leading the North Carolina forces that consisted of sixty whites and sixty Indians. Moore was supposed to march on the 10th to be at Cape Fear by the 17th of August. Captain Robert Screven of the Winyah garrison was to provide piraguas to transport the horses over the river.[298]

Craven had no sooner crossed the Santee River at French Santee when expresses arrived with word that about 700 Indians, mainly Apalachees, had crossed the Edisto River and "began to do mischief."[299]

---

297 Ibid. p. 321 The letter states Craven actually left the Ponds with 100 white men and 100 Negroes and Indians so have may have gathered the rest of his 700 men at Broughton's.

298 Ibid. p. 321 The name of the river was written "Wincaw." BPRO Roll 2 Vol. 6. p. 130 Winyah today is actually the bay that leads to Georgetown, South Carolina, the Waccamaw and other smaller rivers. In the paragraph that follows it states Craven crossed the Santee River.

299 BPRO Roll 2 Vol. 6 p. 130

After the Indians crossed the Edisto River bridge, they were undiscovered until they reached William Livingston's[300] plantation which they burned. Livingston, who may have been the Congregational minister who replaced Archibald Stobo at the White Meeting House in Charles Town in 1704, obtained the 435-acre plantation on Pon Pon (Edisto) River from the estate of Thomas Cochran in 1714.[301] From there, the Indians went to New London where they burned a house. The garrison at New London had a force of fifty or sixty men and the Indians could not capture it so they moved on to the southeast and burned Joseph Boone's plantation house, and a ship he was building. The plantation was located on the mainland on the Dawho River just east of today's Highway 174.[302]

The rampage continued unchecked. Lady Elizabeth Blake's house was burned. She was the daughter of Landgrave Axtell and widow of Landgrave Joseph Blake, former proprietor and governor of South Carolina from 1696 until his death on September 7, 1700. The Axtell property was next to Boone's and Blakes's located on or near Yonges Island on the west side of the Wadmalaw River. The Indians spread themselves along the Stono River and burned

300   In the original letter by Daniell, the name was written incorrectly as "Leviston." BPRO Roll 2 Vol. 6 p. 129

301   The name in the Consolidated Index, p. 18990 is spelled "Levington" and "Levingston." The name is spelled incorrectly on page 233 of *Warrants*, but is spelled correctly, "Livingston," on page 234.

302   BPRO Roll 2 Vol. 6 p. 129

"all before Them" as far as Thomas Farr's. Only Landgrave Joseph Morton's house, on Toogoodoo Creek, escaped being burned.[303] Thomas Farr, who was granted his first land in 1695,[304] owned 430 acres in Colleton County as early as 1704 and later acquired more land. He owned land on both sides of the Wadmalaw River which divides Edisto and Johns islands from the mainland.

There was no battle as the Indians fled in front of Craven's army coming from the north and they retreated across Pon Pon Bridge which they burned. Craven's men repaired the bridge in four or five hours, crossed it, but could not find their enemy. It was speculated that they had returned to their towns and would make raids on the settlers from time to time.[305]

The general agreement is the Indians came within about twelve miles of Charles Town. Four or five white men were killed during the raid. If it were not an exaggeration that all the houses were burned from the Edisto to Mr. Farr's, that is from the Edisto to the Stono, that would mean at least twenty three properties were burned plus the one burned house in New London. There is no indication that the Indians crossed over to Edisto Island.

303   Robert Daniell's letter August 25, 1715. BPRO Roll 2 Vol. 6 p. 129
304   Salley, A.S. *Warrants* Vol. III p. 75
305   BPRO Roll 2 Vol. 6 p. 106 & 131

STONO ISLAND

It was reported the Indians also attempted to cross over to Stono Island on the bridge that led from the plantation that had recently been owned by John Beamer (or Beamor),[306] but the garrison there prevented them from crossing.

Beamer's property, slightly north of the present Dixie Plantation, is shown on the Moll map of 1711 as "Beaman" and located on the west bank of the Stono just north of Farr's property. The map shows that the property across the river from Beamer, located on John's Island, was also owned by Farr.

Where was the Stono Island to which the bridge from Beamer's property supposedly led? Stono Island did exist. Robert Cole and James Williams were each granted land there in 1707 and John Stanyarne obtained land there in 1733. A late mention was in 1752. And Johns Island was recognized as an entity as well. Land was granted on Johns Island from

306   Daniell wrote the name as Reamors. BPRO Roll 2 Vol. 6 p. 129 Larry Ivers *Colonial Forts* p.74 stated the name was Beamer which is correct. No Reamor is listed in the Consolidated Index.

1705 to 1710 to the Stanyarnes, Ravens, Torquets and Mrs. Elizabeth Godfrey. Earlier land grants were made as well.

Johns Island historian Elizabeth Stringfellow states Stono Island, now a part of Johns Island, was the land between the Kiawah River and the Abbapoola River which used to flow into Cole's Creek which flowed into Bohicket Creek. Part of the river and creek were filled in the 1930s or 1940s and Stono Island ceased to be an island.

The bridge, according to Moll's map, could not have led from Beamers former property to Stono Island, but instead to Johns Island.

Because the Stono Indians lived on the southern part of Johns Island as late as 1711, it is possible that some early settlers referred to Johns Island as Stono Island.

MORE GOVERNMENT ACTION

Act 354, ratified on August 27, 1715, made it illegal to export European goods, corn and peas, raw hides, tanned leather and Negro slaves and the act ordered "due care be taken care of and sufficient provision made for sick and wounded persons" and likewise for those who had been made poor by the war. The act would expire March 28, 1716.[307]

Act number 355, also ratified on August 27, 1715, provided that the government would raise £30,000 by stamping bills of credit. At the same time a tax would be imposed to erase the debt of the £30,000 of credit notes. The inhabitants would be taxed on their real and personal estates. "Enquirers and Inquisitors" were appointed to go out and inventory each person's estates including cash and livestock. Men were appointed from each parish. For example the three appointed from St. Philip's parish in Charles Town were Andrew Allen, merchant, Francis La

---

307   Ibid. p. 627

Brasseur and Captain Thomas Hepworth, lawyer.[308]
It was up to the assessors to set the actual tax.[309]

These men, possibly not too popular, must have
been very busy for the next sixteen month as each
assessed all the property and possessions of his
neighbors.

Act 356, ratified on March 24, 1716, made some
interesting provisions for the Tuscarora Indians. "The
Tuscaroras viewed the eruption of the Yemassee
War as a method to obtain revenge against the
Yemassees who had helped defeat them in North
Carolina. Many of them chose to take up arms against
the Yemassee coalition. White South Carolinians
rejoiced."[310] In August 1715, the Commons House
of Assembly decided to reward the Tuscaroras and
proposed such laws that were ratified seven months
later as part of Act 356.[311] When the Tuscaroras
returned to North Carolina after the Yemassee War,
each one was to receive one good trading gun and
a hatchet. Should any Tuscarora be killed in South
Carolina's defense, a Tuscarora slave, who would
have been brought to South Carolina at the end
of the Tuscarora War, would be taken from a white

---

308   McCord, David, *Statues* Vol. II p. 627/628
309   Ibid. p. 628
310   Ramsey, William L. SCHS *Magazine* Vol. 103 (January 2002) p. 57
311   McCord, Davis *Statues at Large* Vol. II p. 634 - 641

master. That slave would be allowed to return to North Carolina, so to speak, as a replacement for a dead Tuscarora. The Tuscaroras were also promised that for every enemy Indian prisoner brought in as a slave that the governor, deputy governor or commander-in-chief would take a Tuscarora slave from a white master and that slave would be made free. In both cases, the slave would be appraised by one justice of the peace and two freeholders and the slave owner would be reimbursed.[312] These provisions of Act 356 "transformed the Yemassee War in one small corner of the Carolinas into a war of liberation."[313]

---

312   Ibid. 636/637
313   Ramsey, William L. SCHS *Magazine* Vol. 103 p. 57

THE WAR AT SEA

One of South Carolina's principal waterways was the inland passage, a connecting link of rivers and creeks that separated the coastal islands from the mainland. A boatman, who was familiar with its branches and tides, could navigate his small boat between Charles Town and Florida and seldom go into the open sea. The inland passage was also used by raiding parties of Spanish and Indians to slip in, strike a plantation and slip out again. This was the route the hostile Yemassee Indians used after they were driven from South Carolina to Florida in 1715. They came up on this sea route often to murder and torture white South Carolinians and steal slaves until their defeat in 1728. The residents of Granville County bore the brunt of these raids. The militia could defend the passage, but only when it knew the enemy was there.[314]

As early as 1685, the province realized the importance of protecting the inland passage. Small

314   Ivers, Larry E *Scouting the Inland Passage 1685 – 1737* SC Historical Society *Magazine* Vol. 73 p. 117 to 129

detachments of soldiers called "watches" were stationed in lookouts, usually a small hut or perhaps a crude tower on coastal islands. The job of the watch was to fire a cannon, light a beacon or carry a message by canoe to the South Carolina militia upon the approach of a Spanish or Indian raiding party.[315]

In 1703, with the constant fear of the Spanish in St. Augustine in mind, the assembly voted to purchase three piraguas made of cedar timbers and planks, each to have twenty oars. A small dory was also ordered. It was approved that "one and twenty" men were to be raised to man the piragues. Apparently the twenty-first man was to be in command.[316]

After 1707, the scout watch patrolled the inland passage in a "scout canoe" which was fitted with sails and oars. The scout was initially authorized to consist of four whites and six Yemassee Indians supervised by Captain Thomas Nairne.[317]

By 1713 the "Port Royal Scouts," then supervised by Henry Quintyne, had proved so efficient that it had superseded, although not entirely replaced, the lookouts as the primary method of guarding the inland passage. They patrolled between Port Royal

315   Ibid. p. 119
316   Salley, A.S *Journal of the Common Assembly* 1703 p. 89
317   Ivers, Larry E. *Magazine* Vol. 73 p. 121

and Spanish Florida, a distance of 120 miles. During that year a second scout canoe was stationed on Johns Island under the supervision of John Fenwick to patrol between the Stono River and Port Royal.[318]

Fenwick, who was born in England about 1675, was in South Carolina by May 8, 1703, when he was appointed an assessor for the area southeast of the Wando River. He had a distinguished military and political career. In 1706, he was a captain and company commander, who with William Cantey, led their companies against the French, who had landed in Christ Church parish. Their troops inflicted nineteen French casualties and captured thirty-three men. He was a major in 1707, a colonel by 1712, active in the Yemassee War and during the 1740 War of Jenkins' Ear, he was made a major general and placed in command of all the provincial provinces. He resided in Colleton County and in 1730 built Fenwick Hall on Johns Island. He returned to England in 1744 because of bad health. He died there two years later.[319]

Scouts were like marines. They could fight from their boats or fight on land. Each man's weapons included a musket, paper wrapped cartridges in a

318 Ibid.
319 Edgar, Walter, Editor *Biographical Directory of the South Carolina House of Representatives* Vol. II p. 244

leather box, and a bayonet, cutlass or light hatchet. Scouts were born and raised on the frontier and were at home on the water and in the woods, but they were a shiftless sort of men who had to be closely supervised.[320]

The most common type of scout boat was the large canoe, a speedy offspring of the Indian dugout. A canoe with ten oars probably had a length of about 35 feet and a beam about six feet. Canoes less than 30 feet in length apparently carried only one mast while longer craft probably had two "gaff-rigged" masts. Oars were the main propellants.[321]

Canoes, piraguas and the whaleboat were converted into scout boats or militia galleys by the installation of additional oars and blunderbusses or swivel guns.[322]

The sea scouts, who proved a major asset in the opening days of the Yemassee Indian War, were ready to continue the fight. Larry Ivers wrote that the scouts were involved in frequent skirmishes after July 1715. Captain Burrows and his crew, in a whaleboat, barely escaped six pursuing canoes full of Indians at Port Royal in late July. His scout force was hurriedly reinforced with six piraguas and

---

320   Ivers, Larry E *Magazine* Vol. 73 p. 122
321   Ibid. p. 122
322   Ibid.

100 men.[323] Burrows had apparently recovered from his wounds received on the opening day of the war.

On October 7, 1715, Samuel Eveleigh wrote a letter in which he stated that Colonel Fenwick received information that on an unspecified date that the Indians were burning plantations in the area of the Combahee River. These actions, and those that follow, could have taken place in July because Eveleigh also wrote about the battle of Daufuskie Island that is generally agreed to have occurred at the end of July.

Eveleigh wrote that Fenwick, upon hearing the news, marched to Pond Bridge,[324] repaired it and marched toward the Combahee River. He then learned the Indians were at John Jackson's house, on the west bank of the Edisto River, near the ferry. Fenwick turned around and perhaps marched his troops through the night to attack the Indians the next morning at daybreak. Out of sixteen Indians, four were killed and two were taken as prisoners with a loss of one white man and one black wounded.

---

323 Ibid. p. 124
324 Since Fenwick lived in Colleton County, this was probably Pon Pon Bridge over the Edisto near present Jacksonboro. It would have been out of his way to cross over Slann's Bridge up by the "Ponds" near the headwaters of the Ashley River.

Fenwick captured four of their piraguas loaded with provisions and plunder.[325]

After the exciting success of capturing four Indian piraguas, Fenwick immediately advised John Palmer, captain of a scout piragua, to lay in wait at the mouth of the Edisto River for three other Indian piraguas still in the river. After a night of probably swatting mosquitoes in some place like Pierre Creek or Big Bay Creek off the North Edisto, Palmer attacked the Indians and captured their piraguas. The Indians leapt overboard and swam ashore.

Palmer then made his way to Port Royal Island where he found William Stone, captain of another piragua, and Burrows with his whaleboat. Stone and Burrows told Palmer there were eight or ten Indian piraguas in the area and the three of them hurriedly departed to Daufuskie Island just south of Hilton Head Island. The Indians had to pass Daufuskie.[326]

The sea scouts had to wait two days before they spotted eight Indian piraguas coming toward them. Stone and his men went ashore and lay in ambush where the Indians had to come ashore if they jumped overboard again. As soon as the Indians had rounded the point, Palmer caught up with them

---

325   BPRO Roll 2 Vol. 6 p. 118
326   Ibid.

and the Indians, seeing him coming, immediately threw their guns into the river and leapt overboard swimming to the place where Stone and his men lay waiting. Of the thirty-seven Indians that were in six of the piraguas, thirty-five Indians were killed and two were taken prisoner. The Indians from the two other piraguas ran into the woods naked and escaped without weapons.

One of the prisoners[327] told the scouts the Yemassees were settled on the Sappola (Altamaha) River in present Georgia. Eveleigh said Robert Daniell was outfitting several piraguas to go and drive them from that area.[328] Daniell and his men did go, but the information proved unreliable and the Indians were not there.

Sometime prior to March 15, 1716, the South Carolinians, who landed a force in Florida where the Euhaws were building a town near St. Augustine, conducted a surprise attack. They captured the Euhaw king, all of his family and thirty of his people[329] who were `taken to Charles Town, sold into slavery and exported to Barbados.[330]

---

327 Larry Ivers wrote the prisoner who gave the information, under threat of death, was an old white haired warrior. He said the Huspahs had settled near the Altamaha River, and the information was eagerly received because it was thought it was the Huspahs who started the war. The Indian was dead by the time Daniell returned. SCHS *Magazine* Vol. 73 p. 125

328 BPRO Roll 2 Vol. 6 p. 118

329 BPRO Roll 2 Vol. 6 p. 159/60

330 Ivers, Larry SCHS *Magazine* Vol. 73 p. 125

While the Sea Scouts were making an important contribution to the defeat of the hostile Indians, the focus of the war was turning northward and westward.

THE CHEROKEES, THE TURNING POINT OF THE WAR

For South Carolina to ensure its safety, it had to have the strong Cherokee nation on its side. The nation had wavered for months on whether or not to join the Yemassee and other Indians or to side with South Carolina. There had been no widespread hostility from the Cherokees but they had murdered some Indian traders.

After August 25, 1715, two men were sent to the Cherokees to "endeavour a reconciliation" between the Cherokees and South Carolina.[331] They were promised £500 if they persuaded the Cherokees to join in an alliance. They were each paid £50, apparently in good faith, from the £500 that might be due them. One of the men sent was Eleazer Wiggan, who survived the opening of the war and who would still be trading with the

---

331 BPRO Roll 2 Vol. 6 p. 156. Theodore Jabbs in *The South Carolina Colonial Militia* wrote two Indian traders volunteered to present South Carolina's case to the Cherokees. p. 305

Indians in 1733.[332] It seemed the two emissaries had succeeded when they returned with about 120 Cherokees with whom the government could personally negotiate a peace treaty. There must have been some apprehension among the residents of Charles Town that during the height of the Indian war a great number of Indians were among their midst. The Cherokees gave the South Carolinians all assurances of their fidelity and agreed, as the English requested, they would attack with their full strength any Indian nation that was an enemy of South Carolina.[333]

After the meeting in Charles Town, a South Carolina "army," part of which was to have joined with a large number of the Cherokees, was sent to Savano Town. There part of the South Carolinians and the Cherokees were to attack the upper Creeks while the rest of the army was to attack the lower Creeks. However, the Cherokees failed to rendezvous and the South Carolina army withdrew. Once again doubts were raised about Cherokee loyalty.[334]

Still trying to win the allegiance of the Cherokees, a bold plan was formulated in November. Col. Maurice

332   City of Charleston *Yearbook* 1894 p. 334 n. 3 BPRO Roll 2 Vol. 6 p. 107
333   BPRO Roll 2 Vol. 6 p. 156
334   BPRO Roll 2 vol. 6 p. 156/157

Moore[335], with 300 paid volunteers, including two companies of blacks, was ordered to march into the heart of the lower Cherokee settlements to seek a treaty. "They were not to go as invaders, but as a reinforced diplomatic mission."[336] The success of this mission was vital to the well being of South Carolina.

---

335 Ibid. p. 157
336 Jabbs, Theodore *South Carolina Militia* p. 306

COLONEL GEORGE CHICKEN'S JOURNAL

Colonel George Chicken was one of the men to go on this expedition to the Cherokees. A journal describing the march, which is attributed to Chicken, survives.[337] This description of the expedition is taken from Colonel George Chicken's journal as copied by Langdon Cheves for the 1884 *Year Book* of the City of Charleston.

The journal began November 27, 1715, and ended February 18, 1716. Entries from December 3 to December 18 were torn out.

On November 27, Chicken left his 1,150-acre plantation, later known as Cedar Grove, which was located near Moncks Corner, and rode to Boochawe House, the plantation of General James Moore. The two of them attended church at St. James Goose Creek and heard the Reverend Francis LeJeau preach. They had dinner after church at Arthur Middleton's and then set out with Captain Nathaniel

---

337   City of Charleston *Yearbook* 1894 p. 315 – 354

Broughton and Captain Thomas Smith, third son of William Smith, and a colonel by his death in 1724. They all arrived at the Ponds about 6 o'clock.

By four o'clock the next afternoon, November 28, Governor Charles Craven and some the gentlemen from town and General James Moore, with gentlemen from Goose Creek, all arrived at the Ponds. Major John Herbert, who had served in the Tuscarora War, came from Wasamsaw, northwest of present Summerville, with the North Carolina men and "part of the norrode forses." Cheves also identifies the "norrode forses" as troops from Virginia.

If there were Virginia forces in this expedition, those "poor ragged fellows" got a grand tour of South Carolina and Georgia during the march. The Virginia forces did not return to Virginia until about March 15 so it is quite possible they were included.

On Tuesday, November 29 Colonel Maurice Moore marched three hours or approximately ten or twelve miles from the Ponds with part of the forces and crossed the Edisto about where Givhans Ferry State Park is located. The next day Governor Craven returned to Charles Town and General James Moore and Colonel Broughton went to the

Edisto River and left Chicken to bring Captain John Cantey's company across the Edisto. This was the same John Cantey who fought with Barnwell in the Tuscarora War.

On Friday, December 2 Colonel John Fenwick arrived with some of the Colleton County regiment. This completed the army of 300 men.

The companies were headed by Broughton, Smith, Daniell and Cantey from Berkley County, Bull and Scott from Colleton County, and Herbert and Hastings from North Carolina. Pight's and Ford's companies of blacks joined them.

Even though pages are missing from Colonel Chicken's journal, it would appear the army averaged about 12.5 miles per day. It was freezing cold some days and the hardest task was fording creeks and rivers. One creek was very steep on each side and several men fell off their horses. Although Chicken did not mention it as such, the Savannah River was crossed on Christmas Day. According to Chicken, the river was half a mile wide with such a strong current several men were knocked off their feet and one man was drowned. His name was "Daues" (possibly Dawes), a pipe[338] maker, who lived with

---

338 A pipe can be something with which you smoke tobacco or a cask for water, wine, etc.

John Barksdale in Christ Church Parish. Another day they crossed four creeks. Later at Horse Creek, which was very deep, they were forced to unload the horses and swim them over. On the return, it took two hours to cross a branch of the Savannah River.

Food was supplemented by hunting en route. One night five white men killed one young bull and one cow while the Indians killed one deer. Many deer were killed as well as turkeys and the Cherokees gave them "Barbyque" venison. On February 11, a buffalo was killed. Cheves wrote this was the only contemporaneous account he had seen of killing buffalo in South Carolina.

On December 29, the men finally marched into their destination, Tugaloo, where Indian men, conducting a peace ceremony, greeted them. The expedition had finally reached its destination. The Indians, who were wearing eagle tails, would invoke the holy name of Yo-he-wah with many incantations while the white men drank the cassena.[339] The young warriors, painted with white clay and crowned with

---

339 Cassena (or cassiny) is made from the leaves of a certain tree boiled in water. The author did not know from what tree the leaves came. Among the Indians only the great warriors or those famous for noble actions were permitted to drink it. Carroll Vol. 2 p. 69/70 John Lawson in *A New Voyage* p. 97 says the Yaupon was called cassena by the Indians. It was used to make tea, grew on the coast and sold to the westward Indians at a high price. Cattle, sheep and deer "delighted in this plant."

swan down, danced before them waving their large fans of eagles' tails, the emblem of peace. After this there was more cassena and then the army marched into the town where the Indian men made a lane to the round or council house, usually raised on a mound. There the conjurer, as the traders called the high priest and great medicine men, greeted them. This Cherokee conjurer was a great friend of the English and greatly esteemed by them.[340] The white men stood back and the conjurer came forward with his hands open to receive the two white flags of truce the English had brought. The conjurer took the flags and he gave them to one of his men so that it would be placed on top of the council house. Then a meal was served until eight o'clock.

The next day all seemed to go fairly well. The conjurer assured the English they would never fight them again, but they would not fight against the Yemassees because they were their "ancient people." They would fight only the Savanos, Euchees and Apalachees. As previously stated, when asked if he would fight the "norrode" Indians, the conjurer replied they had been in Virginia and the governor (Spotswood) had given each Indian a coat, a gun and a blanket and promised to trade with them if they remained "still and quiet" and not come down

---

340 The Cherokees called them "Cheera-ta-he-ge" meaning "Possessed of the Divine Fire."

to fight anymore English. On December 31, the conjurer sent a message to the chiefs of the Creeks to come within fourteen days and talk to the English concerning peace and to bring the white prisoners with them. The conjurer also told them that since the army's departure from Edisto, a white woman had been captured by the Savanos and taken to the Creeks. He also stated that about the end of August fifty Cherokees traveled for four days down the Tennessee river, engaged the Coeakeas (perhaps Kiokees or Keyokees), killed fifty of their men and sixteen French men. The Cherokees took all the women and children as slaves and also they captured many goods the French were going to trade with the Coeakeas. The story about the Coeakeas would be told to show the Cherokees had killed enemies of the English.

On January 1, 1716, it was decided colonels Moore and Herbert, with about twenty-four men, would march to the Cherokee town of Chote, a town of peace or refuge. They arrived there the next day.

After the Indians had painted themselves, the Indians and English together marched into the town where they were met by headmen of Chote and most of the towns from the other side of the hills. They were greeted with an "abundance" of ceremonies including the firing of their guns, waving fans of eagle tails and dancing. Caeser, a chief of the Overhill Cherokees, was telling the young men of his trip to Charles Town,[341] the promises he had made to the governor and why it was necessary to war with the Creeks. The young Indians got so wound up they danced war dances all night.

On January 3, the great medicine man of Cusauwaichee,[342] told the whites that ever since he had known white men he loved them as if they were his children. There were two white men in his town that he had kept alive, but one day he went hunting and two Abequas came in his absence and killed them.

The Cusauwaichee medicine man stated one reason the Indian wars broke out was that Alexander Long, an Indian trader, told the Cherokees the Carolina government was going to make war with the Cherokees and kill all of their head warriors. Long told them he was fleeing Carolina because he could not bear to see it. If Long did tell them that, it was because he wanted revenge.

---

341 This might indicate that Caesar had returned with the first expedition.
342 The traders called the High Priests or great medicine men of the Indians the Conjurer. The Cherokees called them "Cheera-ta-he-ge or "Possessed of the Divine Fire."

Long was fleeing because he feared punishment from the Indian commissioners. On May 5, 1714, the commissioners had found Alexander Long and Eleazer Wiggan guilty of encouraging the Cherokees to attack the Euchees and announced their licenses would be taken from them.[343] The attack against the Euchees, which occurred possibly as early as 1711, was allegedly caused because the Euchees had abused Long and torn his hair out. Henry Hartford, a witness, told the commissioners he had heard some Cherokees say they were incited by Long to attack the Euchees. The commissioners believed the testimony against Long and Wiggan. One source states Long did flee the province[344] and he is not mentioned afterwards in the *Journals of the Commissioners of the Indian Trade*.

The medicine man also claimed that about four to six weeks prior to the outbreak of the war a John Horwood[345] and some friendly Indians had told the Cherokees the English were going to attack them. He also said the traders had been very abuseful to them which was unusual. All of this made the Cherokees believe the English were going to attack.

---

343   McDowell, William L. Jr. *Journals of the Commissioners of the Indian Trade 1710 – 1718* p. 55
344   *1894 City of Charleston Yearbook* p. 334 n. 4
345   He lived in Goose Creek in 1713. A John Harwood was buried in Charles Town March 11, 1729,

The medicine man added he would be the first to attack any who attacked the English. Somehow the medicine man, or so he claimed, missed the fact a large delegation had gone the past September or October to Charles Town and he wished he had known so he could have gone too.

Around nine o'clock in the evening on January 3, there was a great discourse among the warriors in the round house. It was decided that if the Creeks did not arrive within two days, the Cherokees would send the red stick through the nation and prepare to go to war against them. Remember, the notice had only been sent to the Creeks on December 31 and they had been given until January 13 or 14 to arrive.

On January 5, James Alford sent a letter by Jonathan Chester, Indian trader and interpreter, to the Chickasaws in which he stated he understood that some white people were alive among them. In a very conciliatory manner, Alford continued that he believed the claims of the Chickasaws that they had no hand in murders of other white people. Alford advised them that peace had been made with the Cherokees and it was expected that soon the Creeks would also make peace. He urged the Chickasaws to go to Charles Town to discuss trade and peace and take with them some of the headmen of the other tribes. The Chickasaws replied they were very sorry for those misfortunes that had happened to the English in South Carolina. They said if had they known in advance they would have prevented the war from beginning, and that they wanted to live in peace with the English.

The Chickasaws waited some time but did go to Charles Town. About seventeen of them were there in December 1717. James Alford and Alexander Mckay gave a report of the negotiations to the Common House of Assembly, including the fact the Chickasaws would establish a trading house at their town of Coosattes that is about 500 miles from Charles Town. Some of the Chickasaws were summoned to the meeting and Colonel Mckay spoke in Creek to one of the Indians who could translate that into the native tongue of the Chickasaws. The Indians wanted their goods at the same rate that the Cherokees paid, for example, four skins for a pair of stockings. On December 4, 1717, the Commons House of Assembly agreed to open a trade with the Creeks and Chickasaws and ordered Alford, effective January 1, be paid £8 ten shillings per month for his service as interpreter and assistant factor at Savano Town.[346]

Between January 6 and the 23, 1716, the time was mainly spent waiting for the Creeks to arrive.

346   McDowell, William L *Journal of the Commissioners of the Indian Trade 1710 – 1718* p. 240, 242

During this time Wiggan and Doctor Conyers[347] traveled to Tohowee where there was a great "ball play" among the Indians. On the 11th they witnessed another match at Estathoe where those citizens played against Tugaloo.

These games may have been lacrosse since it was popular across the entire Eastern half of the continent. "At each end of a level piece of ground stood two, narrow goalposts, between which a deerskin ball had to be propelled by a hemp-strung or sinew-strung racquet. There were frequently several hundred players on each side, drawn from different tribes. One side would be painted dark and the other light, and there would be many fierce melees and scrimmages with many broken heads."[348]

On a very rainy Monday, January 23, matters began to heat up. Herbert and Chicken were summoned to the Cherokee's war house where the headmen were seated according to rank and "quality." The men asked Caesar and the others why they had been summoned. The Indian replied that they were told by Governor Craven and others in Charles

---

347 John Coniers had a warrant for 500 acres dates April 27, 1704, and John Conniers had a warrant for 500 acres in Granville County dated October 25, 1717. Both entries are indexed as "Conyers, John" in *Warrants for Land* Volume III. Conyers also signed the February 1716/17 Petition to the Crown Against the Proprietors
348 White, John Manchip *Everyday Life of the North American Indians* p. 131/132

Town they were free to go to war against any Indian nations that were "our" enemies. They were told when in Charles Town they could go against the northward Indians and then were told instead to go southward against the Creeks who started the war and had failed to show up and negotiate. The Cherokees were ready to fight.

Chicken tried to dissuade them stating that the Creeks, in the meantime, might have gone down to negotiate with the governor. Then Chicken added an unusual argument stating that if the Cherokees attacked then they could not take any plunder or slaves because the Creeks had not been given enough notice to move their families and possessions. The Cherokees replied they did not want plunder, but only wanted to go to war with them and kill them because it was only recently the English persuaded them to end their war with the Creeks. They said they had given the Creeks fourteen days to come to make peace and that they had failed to show up. The Creeks had been warned that if they did not show up, the red stick would be passed through the Cherokee nation. The Cherokees were going after the Creeks even without the English.

Chicken told the Cherokees they were wrong and the governor had said they could not make war or peace without the permission of the English. The

Indians insisted they had been told they should go against the southward Indians and they had ordered all of their headmen and warriors to meet that day but many still had not arrived because of the bad weather. Chicken asked how many men they had and was told 2,370, half of whom had guns. Chicken tried again to dissuade them not to attack until orders were received. He said Colonel Moore would send a messenger to tell them when to attack. That seemed to satisfy them and Chicken went to bed.

By the next morning, the 24th, the Indians had changed their minds and wanted to send forty-eight of their men to Savano Town for ammunition. Chicken said their warriors should not depart because the Creeks may be delayed because of rumors. Chicken reminded them the arrival of the Cherokees in Charles Town had been delayed because two runaway blacks told them lies and made them afraid to go to Charles Town. The Cherokees would not have gone had not the governor sent two more messengers. Then the real reason was revealed: if the Cherokees made peace with the Creeks, they could not capture them as slaves and without slaves they would not be able to purchase ammunition and clothing. The Cherokees were resolved for war. Finally Chicken once again persuaded them to wait for word from Colonel Moore and he promised word would be sent by one of their own men. Then

Chicken and others left Colonel Moore in Tugaloo. They spent the night of the 26th in Chote.

The 27th of January turned out to be a decisive day. The English received the support of the Cherokees in a very unusual way. As Chicken and his party were preparing to leave Chote, they heard the war whoop coming from Tugaloo and the men rushed to hear what the messenger had to say. Twelve Creeks had entered Tugaloo and eleven had been killed while the survivor was given to a white man to be shot that night. The Cherokees also killed a previously captured Creek who was considered a friend of Colonel Hastings. That evening in Tugaloo the conjurer sent for all the white men to come there to guard the town in the event the Creeks returned with a larger number. The whites agreed as estimates of Creek strength ranged from 200 to 300.

The lower Cherokee wanted to side with the English while the over the hill Cherokees were less certain. The impulsive act of killing the Creek envoys on January 27th put all the Cherokees on the side of the English and they proved to be invaluable allies.[349]

This act ended the great threat that the Cherokees would side with the Yemassees. The Cherokees

---

349 Wallace, D.D. *South Carolina A Short History* p. 89

remained allied with the British until the Cherokee War of 1761. That war was fought in the midlands and upcountry.

THE YEMASSEE WAR WAS NOT OVER

Having won the friendship of the Cherokees, Governor Craven considered he had won the war. In a farewell speech to the assembly in April 1716, Craven reminded its members he had received permission from the Lords Proprietors to return to England. He delayed his plans when the war broke out so that he could make his best effort towards restoring peace and security "to a Province and People for whom I will ever retain the greatest esteem and Affection." Craven added that now the clouds that once threatened ruin and destruction to the province had blown over and their enemies, for the most part, were either defeated or they had fled. He was ready to take his departure. Craven even said the war was "in a manner extinguished."[350]

Thomas Broughton, speaker of the assembly, who had listened to Craven's speech, penned a quick reply, in which he thanked the governor for his kind speech and wished him well, but said he had to take exception to that part of the speech that stated the war was virtually over. Broughton wrote, "it is

350 BPRO Roll 2 Vol. 6 p. 215

the unanimous opinion" of the assembly and the entire province that those "clouds of danger and destruction" were still hanging over them and unless God and the king intervened they would probably cause the ruin of the province. Broughton continued that the "small defeats and disappointments" the Indians had received had not discouraged them from continuing to engage in war with South Carolina.[351]

Broughton stated a large number of Indians were allied with the French in Mobile or the Spanish in Florida and were being encouraged to destroy South Carolina. He pointed out the huge financial expense the province had endured, and would endure in the future because of garrisons that would have to be built and that South Carolina was doing all of this even though it had received no help from the Lords Proprietors. In fact, they felt the Lords Proprietors should have used their power to save and protect their province and should have lobbied the king to help as well, but instead the proprietors seemed to have been the only obstacle to their relief.[352]

Craven had urged the province to remain steadfast in its loyalty to the king. Broughton assured that would happen, but complained that Craven had taken no public notice of disrespectful language used

351 BPRO Roll 2 Vol. 6 p. 211
352 Ibid.

by some people against the king and his succession. This was a reference to the Jacobite sympathizers. It may have also been a slap at William Rhett, who had a picture in his hall of Dr. Henry Sacheverell,[353] a controversial high church Tory, who may have been a Jacobite.

Broughton was also disappointed Craven had not consulted with the assembly about his choice for deputy governor, who would act as governor until Craven's return or until a new governor was named, but Broughton promised to work with whomever was named.[354]

Craven, not the Lords Proprietors, chose Robert Daniell. Craven appointed Daniell deputy governor on April 22, 1716, with full powers under the authority of Craven's own commission. Daniell served until August 10, 1717 when Robert Johnson succeeded him. Daniell is sometimes referred to as governor and other times as deputy governor. He seemed to prefer the title of "governor."

Daniell's name is commonly misspelled with only one "l" as in Daniel Island that he bought on May 12, 1699.[355] It was previously called Thomas Island.

353 BPRO Roll 2 Vol. 6 p.107/8
354 BPRO Roll 2 Vol. 6 p. 213
355 Ibid. Vol. III p. 158

Robert Daniell was in South Carolina by 1677.[356] He obtained two town lots, one in 1678 and the other in 1694. He also owned 500 acres on the south side of the Santee River and 1,000 acres in a location not specified. Daniell's largest land acquisition was on March 9, 1699, when he obtained the entire island of Port Royal.[357] He said it was part of the lands belonging to him as a Landgrave of Carolina.

In addition to having been named a Landgrave of Carolina, Daniell obtained the military rank of colonel and was appointed deputy governor of North Carolina where he served from 1703 to 1705.[358] It is interesting how Daniell actively participated in the early battles of the Yemassee Indian War because he was about 70, then considered a ripe old age. He died in 1718 at age 72. His widow, Martha, married Colonel George Logan.[359] A portrait of Daniell painted by Henrietta Johnston survives. His tombstone is attached to the south wall of St. Philip's in Charleston just to the right of the south doors.

On April 23, 1716, the day Craven sailed from Charles Town, thirty gentlemen sailed in a sloop to

356   Salley, A.S. Warrants Vol. II p. 146
357   Ibid. Vol. III p. 156
358   Raimo, John W. Biographical Directory of American Colonial and Revolutionary Governors 1607 – 1789 p. 427. Mr. Raino spelled Daniell with only one "l."
359   Holcomb, Brent H. South Carolina Marriages 1688 – 1799 p. 154

the bar to "take leave of the governor" who was in a man of war under sail. Four men returned in a different sloop that was overturned and wrecked on a sand bar during a sudden storm. At least two of the four men were drowned: George Evans, who was commissioned by the Lords Proprietors as attorney general March 8, 1707, and served until September 5, 1709[360] and then again from February 21, 1711, until his death. Evans made a will on September 22, 1715, because he was taking a sea voyage to Virginia "and considering the hazards of the sea … do make this my Last Will and Testament;" and Commissary Gideon Johnston who was hindered by gout. In 1707, also impatient to reach Charles Town, Rev. Johnston left his ship at the bar and chose to proceed in a sloop with three other people. He almost drowned upon entering Charles Town harbor. It seems he did not learn his lesson.

Broughton was correct. The war was not over. As early as September 16, 1715, John Tate wrote a letter stating the Indians would not fight a decisive battle, but instead they pursued their old method of bush fighting. He said one of "our" scouts is shot down daily without ever seeing the enemy and with no prospect of revenge by other scouts. The Indians would lie in wait at narrow places in the road where they knew people would pass or lie in bushes near a good spring and when whites would appear "pour

360 *Commissions and Instructions* p. 190

in their volley" and then run off into the woods. Thus they would kill two or three men at a time trying to kill the settlers piece meal. Tate continued that the Indians were all freebooters who carry all of their possessions with them. A little parched corn and puddle water are good for them and fattens them like hogs.[361] Tate was exactly correct. Raids and murders would continue until 1728.

Members of the assembly wrote on January 20, 1717, that they were very sorry to see South Carolina still harassed by the Indians and that their fellow-subjects were being killed daily or that they were being carried away by their savage Indian enemies.[362]

In March 1716 two lieutenants, twenty-five men and a few Tuscarora Indians from North Carolina, were ordered to maintain two scout boats at Port Royal under the command of Major Henry Quintyne, but Captain William Gray assumed command in September 1716.[363] The reason Gray took over is that about August 1[364], Yemassee Indians had raided near Port Royal and captured Henry Quintyne, Thomas Simmons (or Simonds) and Thomas

361   BPRO Roll 2 Vol. 6 p. 122
362   BPRO Roll 2 Vol. 7 p. 9
363   Ivers, Larry Scouting the Inland Passage SCHS Magazine p. 125
364   BPRO Roll 2 Vol. 6 p. 236

Palmenter and tortured them to death.[365] Quintyne had only been granted his land in Granville County in 1714. Palmenter was granted land in 1699 and 1704.[366] Simonds had been an Indian trader but "sold his debts" and had quit trading by March 21, 1712.[367] Another party of Indians captured William Hooper[368] and killed him by degrees, cutting off one joint of his body after another until he died. Dr. Rose, also captured, was left for dead after the Indians cut across his nose with a tomahawk and scalped him, but Rose recovered.[369] In all probability Dr. Thomas Rose was the physician who came from Thame, Oxfordshire, arriving in Charles Town about 1700. He first married Elizabeth the only child of Mr. Bennet of A.K.B. (possibly Accabee). By 1723 Roses' plantation encompassed part of Old Town Plantation where the first South Carolina settlers lived from 1670 to 1680. Rose was buried at Old St. Andrew's Parish on December 3, 1733,[370] seventeen years after being scalped.

Near the end of March 1717, William Steed (or Stead) and one other man were killed at Steed's cattle ranch near the Edisto river bluff and it was

365 Hewatt, Alexander 1836 Carroll Edition *History* Vol. I p. 199
366 SC Archives Consolidated Index Roll 7 p 13777 through 13784 and additionally for Palmenter – *Warrants* Vol. III p. 159 & 192
367 McDowell, W.L. *Journals of the Commissioners of the Indian Trade* p. 20
368 William Hooper may have been the son of Joseph Hooper who was granted 50 aces in July 1695 *Warrants* Vol. III p. 78
369 Hewatt Alexander 1836 Carroll Edition *History* Vol. I p. 199
370 Smith, H.A.M. *Cities and Towns of Early South Carolina* p. 206/207

reported that William Saunders, his wife and some of their family were killed at their plantation.[371]

A few days prior to June 8, 1717, at Mrs. Edwards' island, three male black slaves and one female black slave were lost to the Indians. The white family that was there (It is not clear if Mrs. Edwards was there) made their escape leaving behind good crops in the field for the enemy. Indians also were at Mr. Gibbons' plantation. Both plantations were close to the Port Royal garrison and the writer predicted the frontier would soon be very close to Charles Town.

The constant raids resulted in the disruption of food supplies. Richard Beresford wrote March 29, 1717, the people in Charles Town were ready to eat one another because of a lack of provisions. What they could obtain was very bad and at very high prices. The South Carolina bills had devalued so much no one would take them.[372]

The South Carolina militia was worn out. On June 8, 1717, a writer stated he could not see how it would be possible for a handful of men, exhausted from the war, to continue to protect the province without help from England. He added that Carolina affairs, in relation to the enemy, looked worse than

371   BPRO Roll 2 Vol. 7 p. 17
372   BPRO Roll 2 Vol. 7 p. 17

ever because the Senecas with 1,500 men would join with the Creeks to destroy the Cherokees and Catawbas, allies of the Carolinians, and afterwards destroy the province.[373]

As bad as the massacres were, there were always rumors of even worse events concerning Indians. For example, a citizen writing on August 6, 1716, stated that eighty of the rebels (Scots)[374] had just arrived from Liverpool. As there was a great shortage of fighting men in the province, it was hoped they would be serviceable in the war because several Indian tribes such as the Creeks, Yemassees, Alabamas, Tallabosees, Savanas, etc. were preparing to invade with up to 5,000 men.[375]

Another writer lamented he could not see any end to the Indian war although many people "fancy that it is over."[376]

---

373 BPRO Roll 2 Vol. 7 p. 49 -52
374 These were Scots who were defeated in the 1715 Jacobite uprising and were purchased by South Carolina.
375 BPRO Roll 2 Vol. 6 p. 235
376 BPRO Roll 2 Vol. 7 p. 17

THE WHITES DID NOT JUST FIGHT INDIANS
OR
THE WAR OF THE SLOOP *BETTY*

It has generally been believed that the first time South Carolinians fired on a British war ship was on June 28, 1776, during the battle of Fort Sullivan.[377] That is not correct. South Carolinians, led by Governor Robert Daniell, fired on a British war ship in Charles Town harbor on July 4, 1716.

Governor Daniell and others explained the circumstances in a series of depositions or letters. In a letter written by Daniell July 14, 1716, to the council, he reported it had been "some time since" a Captain Matthew Husson, and his crew of seventy, arrived in Charles Town. The captain had been given a privateer[378] license by the Lord Hamilton

---

377 The fort, located on Sullivan's Island, was later named Fort Moultrie.
378 A license from the government could be obtained to become a privateer who could legally attack and seize enemy ships whether they were merchant or war ships.

which would expire soon. Husson was licensed to capture pirate ships and ships that flew a foreign flag. Husson asked Governor Daniell to renew his license and Daniell most willingly did so and added authority to fight against the Yemassees and other Indian enemies. Husson advised Daniell he would be sailing off the Florida coast where pirates were often found.[379]

Husson obtained information that pirates were "lying amongst" the Bahama Islands. There Husson met a Mr. Perrin from Virginia on board a sloop on which the pirate Benjamin Hornigold sailed. The pirate had taken the ship and its cargo the previous winter from the Spaniards. Perrin pretended to have bought "sundry goods" that Hornigold had on his sloop.[380] Captain Husson immediately seized the pirate's sloop together with a sloop, named *Betty*, which Perrin legally owned. Husson sent Perrin and the goods he purchased from Hornigold in the *Betty* under the command of Mr. Joseph Carpenter, to Charles Town. Perrin would be prosecuted for his clandestine and illegal trade.[381] There is no mention of why Hornigold and his ship were not also taken

---

379   Unless other wise indicated, this entire chapter is taken from the BPRO Roll 2 Vol. 6 pages 190 – 234. These papers are depositions from various people concerning the incident.

380   A sloop is a small fore-and-afte rigged vessel with one mast or a small armed vessel.

381   It was illegal for the British to trade with pirates, the Spanish and the French.

to Charles Town. Later, perhaps in 1717 or 1718, Hornigold was cast away[382] with five other pirates upon rocks located a great distance from the land. Five of the men got into a canoe and were saved.[383] Why was Hornigold not included?

Mr. Carpenter, as ordered, brought the *Betty* into Charles Town Harbor on the morning of Wednesday, July 4, 1716. It can be assumed that July 4, 1716, was a hot muggy day, but Carpenter entered the harbor well before the heat of the day set in.

Coincidentally, this was the same day that the commissioners of the Indian trade met for the first time since April 12, 1715. There was no mention of the war in the minutes of this first day. Those attending were Col. George Logan, Ralph Izard, Esq., Col. John Barnwell and Charles Hill, Esq. Their first meeting consisted primarily of housekeeping items. The commissioners took their oaths, appointed Thomas Lamboll as clerk and bookkeeper and Thomas Barton storekeeper and messenger.

Carpenter anchored about eight in the morning to the southward of the town very near the foot

---

382 Pirates who did not adhere to the pirate's code of conduct were cast away. Sometimes they were cast away because they no longer wanted to be pirates.

383 Johnson, Capt. Charles *A General History ... of Pirates* p. 15/16. Another version is that Hornigold accepted amnesty from the governor of the Bahamas and stopped being a pirate, and his ship later wrecked on rocks where he died.

of Gibbon's Bridge that was owned by merchant William Gibbon. It was also called the lower bridge. The word "bridge" in early South Carolina also meant wharf or pier. Carpenter came ashore to give an account of his actions to Daniell. After Carpenter left, Richard Wigg, the searcher, went on board the sloop and ordered the hatches opened. The searcher was an arm of the Court of the Admiralty and he was legally appointed to search seized ships. The sailors refused to open the hatches stating their orders were to the contrary.

About nine or ten o'clock that morning, Colonel William Rhett, the man who would capture Stede Bonnet the pirate in 1718, and Richard Wigg arrived at Daniell's house just as the governor and Attorney General George Rodd were examining Perrin. Rhett and Wigg informed the governor that the sailors threatened to knock out the brains of anyone who tried to open the hatches of the sloop. The sailors said their orders were from the governor by whose commission the ship was seized. The governor said that was correct and he believed that Rhett pretty well knew the nature of the common seaman whose lack of education may cause the rudeness, but could not justify it.

Daniell said that he would have Captain Nathaniel Partridge, marshal of the Court of the Admiralty, on board the sloop as soon as possible to keep the hatches closed. The attorney general later wrote that Partridge was on board the sloop with a warrant "under the seal of the Court of the Admiralty", and "in possession" of the sloop. Partridge would be fired as sheriff two years hence for letting pirates escape who were under his control.

Rhett insisted on taking the vessel under his custody and that he also take the cargo on shore so that the king's portion might be safe. Daniell replied that he had the king's interest at heart as well and no one else would empty the ship. Daniell thought Rhett and Wigg were content.

Rhett was of a violent and domineering disposition, but the people forgave that for the many good services Rhett provided to South Carolina.[384] Daniell also had an explosive temper and a volatile nature.[385]

Considering the personalities of Daniell and Rhett, it seems very unlikely that Rhett left Daniell's house "contented." Indeed, Rhett went straight from Daniell's to the house of John Brown, a planter, where Captain Howard and Joseph Swaddle were also. Howard was the captain of British war ship,

384 McCrady, Edward *History of South Carolina Vol. I* p. 690
385 Jabbs, Theodore *The South Carolina Colonial Militia* p. 331

the *Shoreham*,[386] that was moored at Rhett's Wharf. Swaddle testified that Rhett vilified and "railed against" Daniell to Howard. Rhett called Daniell an old rogue,[387] old dog, old crooked back, Lurkenburg[388] dog and villain and many other such oaths. Howard was a stranger in town and Rhett, with his railings, eventually persuaded Howard to go with him to the sloop and open the hatches.

There was a large sum of money at stake here. The king, by law, received a percentage of the profits that were brought by the sale of the goods of seized ships. It was not uncommon in South Carolina that the officials of the Court of Admiralty, usually working with the governor, would sell the goods at an inflated rate, but pay the king from the appraised rate.

Rhett was the deputy surveyor of customs and that also gave him a legal right to inspect a seized ship. Contrary to law for one in his position, Rhett

---

386 Also spelled *Shoram* in these depositions.

387 Rogue is defined as someone who gets along in life by cheating, deceiving and taking advantage of others.

388 The only two references to the word "Lurkenburg" on the internet were about this usage by Rhett and that there is a parcel of land called Lurkenburg that is located in Germany near Schlitz (north-east of Frankfurt.) An archivist at the German Archives in Berlin confirmed that and suggested the word might be "Larkenburg," but does not help either. The premier dog organization, the Federal Cynologique Internationale (FCI) located in Thuin, Belgium, has never heard of a breed of dog named Lurkenburg nor have they heard of a town by that name either.

maintained wharves and ships. At one point Rhett was charged with harassing ship owners, who used other wharves and granted favors to his patrons. Rhett had also been criticized because his wife was a merchant.[389] Rhett had a vested interest in getting his hands on the sloop. On the other hand, it would seem Daniell was trying to trump Rhett's position based on the fact Daniell, as governor, had given Husson the license to prey on enemy ships. He would later be accused of issuing a license to any ship owner who wanted to be a privateer. Daniell "tells the people here" that as vice admiral to their lordships of the admiralty board he is equal in power with them and that he sits in the admiralty court as judge.

This "War of the sloop *Betty*" raised a question of authority over who would gain control of the sloop.

Wigg, the searcher, didn't have clean hands either. In May of 1716 a sloop from St. Augustine, with deponent David Bourke on board, arrived in Charles Town. Wigg came on board and seized some of the goods due to a lack of a legal export certificate ("they alleged"). Bourke saw Wigg take some bone lace and he told Wigg that the lace for was for "Mrs. Delamore" and he should not take it. Wigg

---

389 Wallace, D.D. *South Carolina A Short History* p. 123/124

replied, "Take it back for she will scold me more than it is worth." This was not the first time goods were confiscated for "lack of the proper certificate."

Partidge wrote on July 12 that on July 4 he boarded the sloop *Betty*, and had placed the "broad arrow"[390] on the mast of the sloop. Soon after Rhett and Wigg arrived at the sloop in the custom house's boat with those colors flying. At the same time Captain Howard arrived at the sloop *Betty*. His boat was manned and they were armed with small arms and "grenade shells."

Rhett, Wigg, Howard and his crew boarded the sloop. Howard, without saying anything to Partridge, ordered his men to break open the hatches that had been nailed down. Then Howard ordered Wigg to search the contents of the hole which he did and he handed up some of those goods to those on the deck.

At this point George Rodd was "walking in the Bay of Charles Town" when he saw Rhett and the entourage boarding the sloop. Rodd saw goods being removed from the sloop. Pirates had been hanged the day before at Oyster Point at the tip

---

390 Possibly a symbol that meant government had seized the sloop and no one could board it.

of the peninsula and Rodd may have been walking there to check on the bodies.

Partridge and the others still on board heard the governor call out the militia by the beating of a drum. Wigg advised Rhett of the call up and Rhett said it meant nothing to him and he would be happy to fight all the men "the old man" (the governor) could raise. Rhett said he would test "the old man's" power. Partridge reminded Rhett that he seized the sloop prior to Rhett's arrival. Rhett replied that action meant nothing to him. Partridge, being alone among such a large, hostile, armed force, decided he could do nothing more on board. He left the sloop and arrived at the governor's house about two that afternoon of July 4.

Daniell immediately sent for Capt. Matthew Porter, commander of the forts, and the town captains and "ordered the flagg out at Granville Bastion." About 140 of the militia showed up with arms and they were ordered to load their guns. Daniell asked Thomas Hepworth, one of the commanders of the militia of Charles Town, who he thought the governor was — he, or Col. William Rhett. Hepworth replied that Daniell was the only governor. Daniell would appoint Hepworth attorney general by October 2, 1716, to replace Evans who drowned. Daniell left some of his men at Granville Bastion and took Hepworth and his company and they walked to Gibbon's Bridge in the company of William Gibbon. Rhett and Howard were leaving the sloop with confiscated goods, allegedly taking them to the king's warehouse for safekeeping. Daniell shouted at Rhett to stop his actions. Supposedly Rhett could not hear Daniell. But Daniell could hear Rhett in his boat refusing to come ashore and he heard Rhett "huzza" and saw him wave his hat over his head as an act of defiance to the governor and his authority.

Daniell then ordered Captain Porter to first fire a "great gun" from Granville bastion and then, with their small arms, make a running fire at Howard, Rhett and the long boat. Rhett and his party eventually came under cover of the *Shoreham*. During the firing of the small arms, Rhett was shot in his left breast. At first it was thought Rhett would die from the wound, but he did not. The *Shoreham* was moored at Rhett's Wharf with its broadside facing toward the town. Lt. James Fellows of the Shoreham wrote they were in such a bad strategic position because they had not finished filling the ship with its ballast. The militia by then was firing at the *Shoreham* with her colors flying and two or three of the shots "are now in her starboard side." This is documented proof that bullets from the South Carolina militia hit the *Shoreham* — a moment of history. Rhett and his group were able to put the goods on board the *Shoreham*.

Daniell wrote that he decided to go, with his sword sheathed, with George Rodd, to the *Shoreham* and talk to Rhett and Howard. Rodd walked behind Daniell. Daniell left the militia at the upper end of Rhett's Wharf. George Rodd believed that Daniell had come to the wharf to prevent any further escalation of the battle. Lt. Fellows wrote that Daniell approached with his sword drawn and the militia a short distance behind him. Fellows said he had six deck guns ready to fire at the wharf. Fellows advised the innocent people, who were on the wharf watching the drama unfold, to get out of the way. They responded immediately. You can imagine that the whole town turned out for the battle.

Daniell got within five or six feet of the Shoreham when Fellows aimed his musket at the governor, called him an old rogue and warned him that if took one more step toward the ship, he would shoot him. Fellows twice yelled he would ask God to condemn him if he let Daniell on board the ship. Daniell then looked straight at Howard, who was standing near to Fellows. Howard was pointing a drawn sword at Daniell in a surly manner and asked him, "What would you have?" The unexpected reception made

Daniell smile and he turned, without speaking a word, to return to the militia.

As Daniell and Rodd were departing, Rhett attempted to jump off the ship (remember Rhett's fresh gun wound) but was held back by the captain and others. Rhett then proceeded to constantly cry out that he would kill the old rogue and he would kill the old dog. The governor continued to withdraw. He felt it was pointless to argue any further. Rodd was walking behind Daniell because Daniell was walking faster. Then Rhett grabbed a heavy shovel, jumped off the ship and beat Rodd with the shovel. Rhett struck Rodd on the back twice and many other blows to the head with a "design to kill him." Daniell wrote that Rhett hit Rodd with the shovel "with all his might" but Rodd made a move to escape further blows and drew his sword. Daniell wrote that Rodd, who had Rhett's life in his power, spared Rhett's life because of Rodd's good nature.

As previously stated, Rodd died two months later, but there is no known correlation between this attack and his death.

Joseph Swaddle was with the governor at Gibbon's Bridge on July 4 when muskets were fired at Rhett and Howard. Swaddle grabbed a musket from one of the militia and fired three times across the water at Rhett. The gun misfired each time. Lt. Fellows saw Swaddle for the first time after the 4th of July the evening of the 11th at Nathaniel Partridge's house. Swaddle had been turned over to the justice of the peace for not only trying to shoot Rhett three times but for also saying he would shoot Rhett whenever he had an opportunity. Swaddle not only hated Rhett because he wouldn't approve the £50 request from the assembly to repair the *Bachelors Adventure* but because Rhett had seized Swaddle's ship charging he had traded illegally.

Fellows wrote that Swaddle "belonged to the *Shoreham*" and that Captain Howard permitted Swaddle to walk around the quarterdeck.

Fellows told Swaddle of his ingratitude to Capt. Howard. Swaddle said he was not guilty of trying to shoot Howard and that Howard was more obliged to him than he was to Howard. That put Fellows "in a passion" and he struck Swaddle on his face once with the back of his hand. Swaddle immediately hit Fellows several times. Partridge broke up the fight and quickly went to Daniell's house. Partridge brought Daniell back to his house. As soon as Daniell saw Fellows he went into a rage and ordered Partridge, the marshal, to cast Fellows into irons. For two days Fellows and Howard requested and demanded that Fellows be released. Finally on the 13th,

Fellows released himself by a habeas corpus by giving bail for his appearance at the trial and for future good behavior.

Lt. Fellows wrote at the time of the battle he was very concerned about his captain and Rhett when he saw the militia firing at them. It moved him very much. When Fellows saw his majesty's ship fired upon and as he felt the shots strike under his feet where he stood on the gunwale, he saw Daniell and his men coming upon the wharf to attack the ship. Fellows was raised "to the greatest pitch." He felt "his sacred majesty was being attacked in person" and because "I was in a bad posture of defense, I would have been cut to pieces and never would have lived to have seen the ship taken, which would have been nothing but doing my duty."

The goods confiscated by Rhett and Howard were returned to Daniell shortly after July 4. Daniell had Rodd present a brief to the council and the assembly stating that Howard, Fellows and officers and sailors of the *Shoreham* were guilty of high treason and that they should be punished. Council and the assembly rejected the brief.

Who won? Probably Daniell because he got the goods returned to him. He also won because he ordered the South Carolina militia to fire upon a British war ship and he was not convicted of high treason. Remember that under English law a convicted traitor was hanged, but cut down before dying when their bowels were removed and burned. After that their head would be severed from the body and then their bodies would be cut into quarters.

THE CREEKS

By April 1717, the peace process began with the Creeks when two Indians arrived in Charles Town accompanied by Jonathan Chester and another white man. The Indians gave accounts of white people, thought to be dead or enslaved including Mrs. Bull and Mr. Sommers'[391] children. The new assembly met in April and several of its members decided to travel with Governor Daniell to the garrison at the Ponds to meet the headmen of the Creeks to conclude a peace treaty with them. To seal the treaty and to make retribution for their past actions, the Creeks had promised to bring several hundred skins. Some South Carolinians feared this would cause a jealousy among the Cherokees who wanted to make war on the Creeks for their past murders of Cherokees.[392]

---

391 *Warrants for Lands* Vol. III p. 208 & 228 This may have been Thomas Summers who was granted 100 acres in Berkley County in 1707. This may have also been the same Summers mentioned who in 1710 lived near Captain George Hearn.
392 BPRO Roll 2 Vol. 7 p. 18

In June 1717, there was a rumor the Senecas and Mohawks had joined with the Creeks to destroy the Cherokees and Catawbaws. If this rumor were true, the attack never happened. The Creeks made a proposal for peace, supposedly prior to the alliance with the Mohawks and Senecas, and all were to meet at Savano Town on June 6. Only one Creek, named Bocatie, showed up and said the Creeks could not make peace before their corn was ripe. Bocatie said they would not harm the English, but would have no peace with the Cherokees and Catawbaws. The writer said that what the Creeks were demanding was that the South Carolinians not assist the Cherokees or Catawbaws.[393]

In November 1717, a treaty with the Creeks was signed in Charles Town and historian D.D. Wallace stated that act officially ended the war.[394] Also in November 1717, the assembly deemed the war to be over when it declared the public treasurer to be in contempt for attempting to pay army commissioners with only the governor's approval. The assembly had passed an act stating that during the war the governor was allocated a £500 fund he could use at his discretion while the war lasted. When the assembly declared the war was over, the governor could no longer use that fund.

---

393   BPRO Roll 2 Vol. 7 p. 49/50
394   Wallace, D.D. *South Carolina A Short History* p. 90

The governor agreed the assembly was legally correct.[395] The assembly was defending its right to make defensive appropriations and perhaps was a bit hasty in declaring the war over. The war was not over.

---

395 Jabbs, Theodore *Colonial Militia* p. 314`

THE SPANIARDS

A Carolinian wrote in June 1717, that he thought the Spaniards were a greater enemy than the Indians because if they had not supplied the Indians with guns, ammunition, etc. the war would have already been over and a lasting peace in place.[396]

Why were the Spaniards such enemies of South Carolina? In 1494 war loomed between Portugal and Spain because each country wanted to protect its sea-lanes and prohibit the other from intruding. On June 7 that same year at Tordesillas,[397] representatives of the two countries agreed to divide the world using an imaginary line running pole to pole 370 leagues[398] west of the Cape Verde Islands. This gave Portugal everything 180 degrees east and Spain everything 180 degrees west.[399] Among other lands, this gave Spain the entire western hemisphere, except for Brazil that fell within Portugal's domain.

---

396   BPRO Roll 2 Vol. 7 p. 50
397   Tordesillas, a small town on the Duero River, is 18 miles south west of Valladolid and 110 miles northwest of Madrid.
398   A league is a varying measure, usually about three miles, of traveling distance.
399   Burns, E. Radford *Latin America A Concise Interpretive History* p. 13

Thus Spain was able to claim all of North America south of Newfoundland. This huge territory was to become known as "La Florida." Spain took this claim very seriously and it became a consistent policy of Spain to eject interlopers from "its" territory.

Europeans discovered Florida in 1513 under the leadership of Juan Ponce de Leon, but the first permanent European settlement in Florida, St. Augustine, was not established until 1565. St. Augustine, except for the even smaller Spanish settlement of Pensacola, was effectively Florida. In the early days, the names St. Augustine and Florida were interchangeable.

Even though St. Augustine was sacked in 1668 by the privateer, Robert Searles, who rescued Henry Woodward, Spain would not abandon Florida to England. Queen Regent Mariana of Spain allotted an extra 10,000 pesos to construct a fort of stone instead of the usual wood. It is called Castillo de San Marcos. When the queen heard of the founding of Charles Town in 1670, she increased the fort's garrison from 300 to 350 men.[400] St. Augustine's fort, that took twenty-four years to complete, would never be captured by force.

The 1670 Treaty of Madrid fixed the boundary between Spanish Florida and English Carolina at

400   Bushnell, Amy Turner *The New History of Florida* p. 73

about ten miles north of the Savannah River. Port Royal, or Barra de Santa Elena as the Spanish called it, was right on the border. The boundary line was observed more on paper than in practice. In 1670 Florida Governor Zendoya still hoped to remove the English and would not publish the Treaty of Madrid for two years in hopes he would be freer to act. The Spanish Queen in 1671 authorized Zendoya to drive the English away from Santa Elena but without breaking the peace.[401]

In August 1670, right on the heels of the founding of Charles Town, the Spanish came with Indians to attack but withdrew without attacking because of a storm.[402]

In 1684 fifty-one Scots settled on Port Royal Island. They antagonized the Spanish at St. Augustine who in 1686 destroyed the Scottish settlement and moved on in an attempt to capture Charles Town. The militia and another storm saved the province.[403]

South Carolinians cried for revenge, but had to wait until 1702 and the outbreak of The War of Spanish Succession, 1702 – 1713. The English and Spanish colonies could not attack each other when

401 Crane, Verner W. *The Southern Frontier* p. 10/11
402 Wallace, D.D. *South Carolina A Short History* p. 29
403 Ibid. p. 41

England and Spain were at peace. Governor James Moore, with Robert Daniell second in command, 1,200 men, 600 white and 600 Indians, attacked by land and sea and quickly occupied St. Augustine. The Spanish governor, Joseph de Zuniga y Zerda moved the town's population of 1,445 into the fort to join the military garrison of 323 men. The Spaniards exhibited remarkable endurance and determination in spite of horribly crowded conditions. Zuniga's strong leadership was responsible in keeping up morale and hope. Moore never captured the fort. Moore sent to Jamaica for reinforcements and Zuniga sent to Havana for reinforcements. After a two month siege, reinforcements from Cuba arrived first and Moore burned the town, except for the hospital, and withdrew. The withdrawal became a rout and Moore was severely criticized.[404]

After this humiliating defeat in 1702, former Governor Moore decided in 1704 to attack the Apalachee Indians who lived in the panhandle of Florida. By destroying the Apalachees, Florida would be left much more vunerable to the English. Revenge may have been his motive. Moore destroyed the Apalachees, but in doing so he also virtually destroyed the Spanish mission system in Florida. It is not realized how much Moore destroyed.[405]

---

404 Arnade, Charles W. *The New History of Florida* p. 107
405 Ibid. p. 108

THE SPANISH ROLE IN THE YEMASSEE WAR

Even though there was a history of great animosity between Florida and South Carolina, historian D.D. Wallace wrote that the assertion that the St. Augustine Spaniards instigated the war has never been proved. The fact that the Spanish were delighted the war broke out, and that the governor of St. Augustine extended the war for years, is certain.[406] It was reported that when word reached the citizens of Havana that all South Carolinians had been captured or killed by the Yemassees, they showed their pleasure in receiving this news by the ringing of bells, the building of bon fires and other demonstrations of joy.[407] We already saw that when the Yemassees retreated to St. Augustine in 1715, they were received as heroes as though they had won the war. Bells were rung and guns fired to celebrate their arrival.

Historian Alexander Hewatt wrote that for twelve months prior to the outbreak of the war, the

---

406 Wallace, D.D. *South Carolina A Short History* p. 86
407 BPRO Roll 2 Vol. 6 p. 240

chief warriors of the Yemassees often traveled to St.Augustine and returned loaded with presents such as hats, coats and guns and ammunition. Yemassee warriors told John Fraser, a Scottish highlander who lived among the Yemassees, that they had dined with the governor of St. Augustine. They had washed his face, a ceremony used by Indians as a token of friendship, and said that the Spanish governor was their friend, not the governor of Carolina. The South Carolinians were not concerned because they knew the Yemassees' passion for receiving presents.[408]

Hewatt's writings are not documented. A letter that is documented was written by a committee appointed by the assembly that included Benjamin Godin, Ralph Izard and Edward Hyrne, and was presented on August 6, 1716. Their letter reported that the Yemassees captured Hugh Brian, son of Joseph Brian, at the beginning of the war. Brian related he had often heard the Indians telling one another the Spaniards encouraged them to kill the English provided the Indians did not let the Spaniards see what had been done. Brian also witnessed the Spaniards furnishing the Yemassees with whatever they needed to carry on the war. Brian was a captive of the Creeks for more than a year and as such witnessed arms coming in to the Indians from French Mobile and Spanish Pensacola.[409]

---

408   Hewatt Alexander, Carroll 1836 Edition Vol. 1 p. 191/2
409   BPRO Roll 2 Vol. 6 p. 236/7

Brian was finally sent to Charles Town by the "Woospau" (Huspah) king, who had saved him from a cruel death, to work out a peace treaty for the Indians.

Sanute, the Indian who warned Hugh Fraser about the upcoming hostilities, arrived at the Frasers with gifts given him by the Spanish. He told them the English were all wicked heretics and would go to hell, a thought that sounds as if it must have come from Spanish Catholics. The Indians were only waiting for the red stick to be returned from the Creeks so the war could begin and they hoped that the Yemassees, Creeks, Cherokees and many other tribes plus the Spanish would engage in this war. Sanute told the Frasers if they stayed he would see they were not tortured, but as their friend, he would kill them quickly.[410]

Fraser, astonished at this news, asked Sanute how could the Spanish make war on the English when the two nations were at peace. Sanute replied that the Spanish governor told him there would soon be a war against the English and while the Indians attacked by land, the Spanish would send a fleet to Charles Town so no one could escape.[411] The next war between England and Spain was to be the short War of the Quadruple Alliance, August 2,

---

410   Hewatt, Alexander, *History* 1836 Carroll Edition p. 192/3
411   Ibid.

1718 – February 17, 1720. It is unlikely the Spanish governor in Florida could see a war three years in advance. However, during the war of the Quadruple Alliance the Spanish did have plans to send a fleet from Havana to attack Charles Town. In 1719 the French invaded Florida, captured Pensacola and the plan to attack Charles Town was dropped because the Spanish had to defend Florida.[412]

Fraser also asked Sanute when the plan for the Yemassee War began to be formed. Sanute replied it was twelve months prior when Ishiagaska, one of the main chiefs, and four other Indians went to the Creeks and carried with them a Spanish plan for destroying all the English inhabitants of the province.[413]

It is obvious that the Indians and Spanish were courting each other prior to the outbreak of the war. The Indians would have wanted assurances from the Spanish of having arms furnished to them and to have a place of refuge if necessary. The Spanish were happy to oblige. It was a way the Spanish could harass and attack the Carolinians while Spain and England were at peace. The anti English rhetoric the Indians heard in St. Augustine was enough to fuel

412   Arnade, Charles W. *The New History of Florida* p. 109
413   Hewatt, Alexander *History* 1836 Carroll Edition p. 193/4

the fire. Had there been no Spanish Florida, there still may have been a Yemassee War, but it would have been much shorter. Technically, the Spanish did not start the war, but they made it much more possible for the war to begin and the Spanish should be included as one of the causes of the war.

RESENTMENT OF ST. AUGUSTINE

The Yemassees had been driven out of South Carolina. On March 3, 1716, the Lords Proprietors wrote to the governor and council of South Carolina that it was their intent that the tract of land formerly known as the Yemassee settlement would be parceled out to new settlers in proportions not exceeding 200 acres. The settlers would be exempt from paying rent for five years and at the end of the five years a settler could rent or purchase the land.[414] South Carolinians liked that plan, but realized that the threat of Yemassee raids would prevent that. They wanted the Yemassees at St. Augustine totally crushed and asked England to send troops to accomplish that.[415] Then the plan of granting each settler up to 200 acres was rescinded by the proprietors who ordered the Yemassee land surveyed in tracts of 12,000 acres each for themselves. This action was one of the reasons that led to the downfall of the proprietors,

---

414   BPRO Roll 2 Vol. 6 p. 151
415   Ibid. p. 238

By June 1716, the government of South Carolina had received many complaints from its residents about the Spanish inciting and encouraging the Indians to raid, steal property, slaves and cattle and to murder settlers. Governor Daniell appointed Major James Cochran as agent to go to St. Augustine to demand the return of the stolen items and slaves that the Spanish had purchased from the Indians. Cochran, who was dead by March 19, 1722, was a member of the assembly and described by Daniell as, "…a person of known reputation, substance and of good credit in the province."[416] A total of ninety-eight slaves had been stolen in 1715. John Barnwell and William Bray each had nine slaves stolen at that time. An additional nineteen slaves were stolen by the Yemassees in 1720 and 1721.[417]

In St. Augustine, Cochran found slaves of some of his Port Royal neighbors. The slaves said they had been sold by the Indians to the Spanish and, according to Cochran, they begged to be returned to their South Carolina owners. The slaves were not allowed to return with Cochran. George Duccott (or Duckett or Ducat) advised Cochran that when he had been in St. Augustine the Yemassee Indians told him the Spanish supplied them with as much gunpowder and balls as they demanded. Also the Spanish purchased

416   Ibid. p. 244/245
417   Ibid. p. 39

all the stolen goods from South Carolina that the Indians brought.[418]

Duccott himself had applied to the assembly for a £100 reimbursement because a Spanish privateer plundered his ship of its rum, skins and sugar.[419]

By August 6, 1716, the South Carolina government had sent a letter to the governor of St. Augustine demanding his observance of the first articles of the treaty of peace that in 1713 concluded The War of Spanish Succession between Great Britain and Spain. These articles stated neither nation was to give any aid to the enemies of the other. The Spanish governor replied that the Yemassees, who had previously revolted against the Spanish crown, had now returned to their former allegiance and were considered subjects of Spain. Because of that the governor had no choice but to receive them and treat them kindly and to protect them from the English. Also if anyone, free or slave, embraced the Catholic Church, he or she was considered a subject of Spain and would not be sent from Florida without the permission of the king of Spain. This encouraged South Carolina slaves to run away to Florida, a situation South Carolinians hated.

---

418   Ibid. p. 246
419   Ibid. p. 238

The Carolinians argued in their letter that if in peacetime subjects of Spain were allowed not only to "destroy" the subjects of Great Britain but were encouraged and assisted by the officers of the king of Spain, then that was the greatest violation imaginable of the treaty. This was the case with the Yemassees whose only ammunition and provisions came directly from the king of Spain's garrison at St. Augustine. They added that soon the Yemassees would have some of their own food that they planted near St. Augustine after the beginning of the war. They complained that because the Spanish refused to return their runaway slaves that caused even more slaves to escape to Florida. Even worse, the Spanish allowed the Yemassees to keep several white women and children from South Carolina among them as slaves. When the South Carolina agent, James Cochran, was in St. Augustine he only saw two South Carolina children there who, the Spaniards claimed, had been kept so they could make them into good Christians. Various ship captains, who had been in St. Augustine, reported to the Carolinians that the governor in St. Augustine said all Carolina belonged to the king of Spain and he hoped in a short time to see it united with his dominion.[420]

---

420   Ibid. p. 239/240

The Carolinians complained that after all of the kindness they had shown to the Spanish, the Spanish were now encouraging the Indians to kill Carolinians.[421]

The Carolinians further complained that all of this was a "bad return" of the civilities that the Spanish had received from the English. During this correspondence, the 1702 burning of St. Augustine by South Carolinians was not brought up. They said they had prevented the Indians from doing any harm to the Spanish. The South Carolinians, during the War of Spanish Succession, had stopped the Indians from capturing Spanish soldiers and torturing them to death. On July 9, 1712, the commissioners of the Indian trade had issued a list of instructions for the Indian agent. Item eleven provided a reward of £5 to be paid to any Indian who brought in a live Christian prisoner.[422] The reward offered ended the practice of torturing Christian prisoners because the Indians wanted the money.

Prior to this reward, the Yemassee, and perhaps other Indians, would capture Spanish soldiers in Florida, some even from the walls of St. Augustine, and cruelly torture them to death in their towns. Hewatt wrote that when the Indians tortured the

---

421 Ibid. p. 240/1

422 McDowell, William *Journals of the Commissioners of the Indian Trade 1710 – 1718* p. 33

Spanish, sometimes they would cut them to pieces slowly joint by joint with knives and tomahawks. At other times, the Spanish prisoner would be buried up to his neck and the Indians would use the exposed head for target practice with bow and arrow while other unfortunate prisoners were tied to trees and their naked bodies pierced in the most tender places with sharp pointed sticks of burning wood. The latter means of torture was used most frequently because it was the most painful.[423]

---

423   Hewatt, Alexander *History* 1836 Carroll Edition Vol. 1 p. 191

FIGHTING THE "FLORIDA" INDIANS

Now that the Yemassees were considered to be subjects of the king of Spain, South Carolina had to deal with that.

In early 1719 three Creek Indians, who were related to the Huspaw king, proposed that they be allowed to go to St. Augustine. They were certain they could convince the Huspah king, "who first began the Yemassee War." into deserting the Spanish and taking all the Yemassees with him. The Creek Indians believed they could get the Yemassees to make a peace with the English. Colonel John Barnwell, who was in charge of this project, wrote from St. Mary's, Georgia, on Monday, April 20, 1717, that the three Creeks who had gone to St. Augustine on Thursday the 16th had just returned and had not successfully completed their mission. The Creeks had found the Huspah king "in such a temper" they dared not make their proposal to him. The Spaniards had made the king "Chief Generall" of 500 plus Indians and they were to immediately attack the English.[424]

---

424 BPRO Roll 2 Vol. 7 p. 186

The Spaniards carried the Huspah king around the town in triumph with drums and trumpets leading the way. The Indians had already received their ammunition and most were to set out by water on Tuesday the 21st. Seventy of the Indians were to travel by land and thirty of those were to attack Pon Pon. Thirty more were to follow with Spanish or mulatto horsemen.[425] The Spaniards told the Yemassees they would pay the same price for English heads that they paid for horses, explaining that the English were their greatest enemy.[426]

Barnwell wrote, again from St. Mary's, "I am so fatigued and the Merrywings torment me to that degree while I write upon my knees that you may well excuse any imperfections."[427] The Oxford Dictionary states merrywings are a kind of gnat or mosquito found in the West Indies. April 20th is a little early for mosquitoes, but it is prime time for gnats. Barnwell must have been sitting using his thighs and knees as a prop for his paper. It is just as today as people use their thighs as a prop for a laptop.

Barnwell took immediate action to warn the settlements. He sent the whaleboat by sea, but he traveled in his canoe close to land. The whaleboat

425   Ibid.
426   BPRO Rolls 2 Vol. 7 p. 187
427   Ibid. p. 187

was to put in at Port Royal and the crew was to send a canoe to Wilton or to Colonel Palmer where they were to get a horse. He feared the Indians would reach Pon Pon first. Barnwell did take time to write a note to Captain John Beamer, urging him to let young Brian go to Combahee to save his father's slaves. He also wrote a letter to Captain Jackson and also to Major Cochran. Both letters were sent by an express to Colonel Palmer.[428]

Barnwell predated Paul Revere's famous ride by fifty-six years, but there was one big difference. There are no records that this invading army reached South Carolina in April of 1719. Better safe than sorry.

---

428 Ibid. p. 188

RAIDS, RETALIATION AND SEYMOUR BURROWS

It is known the raids did continue. Hewatt wrote that during 1719, "Savage Indians were now and then making incursions into South Carolina settlements and spreading havoc among the scattered families." In September 1719, a scalping party of Indians, probably Yemassees, entered Granville County, surprised Mr. Levit and two of his neighbors and knocked out their brains with tomahawks. Then they captured Mrs. Seymour Burrows, her young child, her man Marcus and Mrs. William Ford and carried them off with them. "The child, finding himself in barbarous hands, began to cry upon which they put him to death before his mother's eyes." Mrs. Burrows began to cry, probably hysterically, and was threatened with death if she did not stop crying. She stopped crying and survived and was taken to St. Augustine. Mrs. Ford and Marcus were unable to travel fast enough to suit the Indians and were put to death.[429]

429 Hewatt, Alexander *History* 1836 Carroll Edition Vol. 1 p. 213/214 & BPRO Roll 2 Vol. 8 p. 94/95

Mrs. Burrows' husband, Seymour, arrived in St. Augustine twelve days prior to the arrival of his wife. Barnwell wrote he was carrying letters from Governor Robert Johnson.[430] Whether Burrows was sent as a mediator to negotiate with the Spanish or whether the governor had written a letter requesting the release of Mrs. Burrows is not clear. Thinking he was a spy, the Spanish made him and his men "close prisoners."[431] His men must have been the crew from the whaleboat.

Upon Mrs. Burrows' arrival in St. Augustine, one of the Yemassee kings declared he had known her since her infancy[432] and that she was a good woman who should be allowed to return to her husband. The Spanish, while refusing this request, rejoiced with the Indians in the number of scalps brought with them from South Carolina. Burrows was released from prison because he was ill and he and his wife were reunited in Captain Romo's house. Barnwell wrote Burrows was expected to recover, but Hewatt wrote he died. He probably died in Captain Romo's house.[433] Thus the hero of the opening day of the Yemassee War died in St. Augustine.

---

430   Gov. Johnson served August 10, 1717 to December 21, 1719.
431   BPRO Roll 2 Vol. 8 p. 95
432   Since one of the Yemassee king's knew Mrs. Burrows since infancy, it is possible she was an Indian.
433   Hewatt, Alexander *History* 1836 Carroll Edition Vol. I p. 213/214 & BPRO Roll 2 Vol. 8 p/ 94/95

Mrs. Burrows survived and returned to South Carolina to tell her saga to Governor Johnson. She said the Huspah king, who abducted her, told her he had orders from the Spanish governor to spare no white man, but to bring alive to St. Augustine every captured black slave for whom they were to be paid a reward. She said this policy was to encourage the Indians to harass South Carolina.[434]

John Barnwell wrote a report to Governor Johnson about an expedition that departed on September 28, 1719, to attack the Spanish and Indians at St. Augustine. This expedition, which departed in seven canoes filled with ammunition and provisions, consisted of fifty Indians, Melvin, a white man, and two half breeds named Musgrove[435] and Griffen. Oweeka, a Creek, was the general and Wettly (or possibly Hettly), a Palachucola, was second in command. They arrived at St. John's River on Saturday, October 10 where they left their canoes and proceeded on foot taking a circuitous route to avoid being detected.[436]

Even though one of the invading Indians, not obeying orders, alerted the Yemassees and the Spanish, the attack proceeded. Three Indian towns at once were

434   Hewatt, Alexander *History* 1836 Carroll Edition Vol. I p. 214
435   This may have been Johnny Musgrove, interpreter and trader, one-half Indian son of Colonel John Musgrove. From *South Carolina Indians & Indian Traders* edited by Theresa M. Hicks p. 127
436   BPRO Roll 2 Vol. 8 p. 92

attacked but only twenty-four Indians were taken prisoner and only five or six killed because most had fled with the advance warning. The Indian houses and provisions were burned and plunder was taken. In Tuloomata, a Euhaw town within a mile of the castle at St. Augustine, one of the three towns attacked, a "fine" church was burned and its plate taken along with some of the friar's domestics. The friar, Pedro de la Lastras, also had his possessions in his house plundered, but the house was not burned.[437]

The attacking Indians also went to the Palatchee town, four miles from St. Augustine, because the Palatchees had promised to revolt and join in the attack. Their town was deserted. By the time their corn, houses and roundhouse had been burned, the "sun was two hours in the sky" and fifty or sixty Spanish soldiers were spied in full march after the attacking Indians. Apparently the Indians eluded the Spanish soldiers. The Indians decided that a Spanish soldier, who had been captured during the night, would be sent with a flag of truce to the Spaniards. He was to tell them they had no quarrel with the Spaniards, but, instead, they were there to punish the Yemassees who had captured Mrs. Burrows and the others. This is only the mention of the purported mission of the expedition. Some of the Indians had stripped the prisoner, who was to carry the flag of truce, stark naked. When he approached the

---

437   Ibid. p. 92/93

other soldiers they thought his nudity was a sign of contempt, ignored him and immediately fired a volley at the Indians 400 yards away.[438]

Deciding not to flee and lose their slaves and plunder, the Indians attacked the Spanish by dividing into two groups, each of which would attack a flank. The heavily weighted Spanish soldiers, who fought closely together, were no match for the nimble Indians who killed fourteen and took about ten prisoners during the Spanish retreat. About seven of the prisoners were stripped naked and released to return to St. Augustine and the remaining three were taken to South Carolina along with twelve slaves.[439] The two canoes carrying the Spaniards and the slaves arrived at John Barnwell's house on Sunday, October 25. One Spaniard seemed to Barnwell to be a mestizo[440] and the other, who was naked, not to be white. The latter prisoner had lived in St. Augustine for sixteen years and had a wife and eight children. Barnwell told the Indians to take the prisoner to Charles Town because he had no clothes to give the prisoner. Barnwell did not report what happened to the mestizo. The remainder of the expedition reached Barnwell's house the next

---

438   Ibid. p. 94
439   It is not clear if these slaves were captured Indians or whether they were returning stolen Negro slaves.
440   *Webster's Dictionary* "a person of mixed parentage, esp. one of Spanish or Portuguese and American Indian descent."

day.[441] It is very interesting that Barnwell had no clothes to spare.

Barnwell wrote that one of the Spanish prisoners informed him that Monsieur La Hay, a French privateer, had brought three captured English ships, carrying cargos of sugar, cotton and molasses, and the three captains and thirty-one sailors into St. Augustine. The captured crews were in prison there. La Hay had bragged he would kill all the Indians invading St. Augustine and either led or sent ten or sixteen of his best men in the attack previously described.[442]

The War of the Quadruple Alliance, in which England, France and others were allied against Spain, had not yet ended. Why would a French privateer capture ships of England, France's ally and take them to an enemy Spanish port? Perhaps La Hay was more of a pirate than a privateer.

Barnwell ended his 1719 report with a very significant statement, "I congratulate with your honor, Governor Johnson, this dawning of quietness to our poor Southern parts ..."[443] The Yemassee War was slowly becoming part of history. But it was not over with either the Spanish or the Yemassees.

---

441   BPRO Roll 2 Vol. 8 p. 94/95
442   La Hay's "best men" did not perform well in the battle.
443   BPRO Roll 2 Vol. 8 p. 96

In 1722, more than two years after the end of the War of the Quadruple Alliance, South Carolinians were complaining the Spanish were still seizing English ships and taking them to St. Augustine. Since the cessation of arms, ten English ships had been seized with cargos of slaves, rum, rice and other items. One ship had 1,500 pieces of eight on board. Values of the cargos of the seized ships ranged from a high of £3,050 sterling to a low of £100.[444] The Spanish were operating right off the coast of South Carolina.

In 1726 and 1727, the Yemassees stepped up their raiding in South Carolina and were continuing to murder whites and carry off every slave they could find. Hewatt states the Spanish did allow a compensation to the South Carolinians for their losses, but few ever received it.[445]

On June 13, 1728, thirteen years after the outbreak of the Yemassee War, John Palmer was appointed by council, with the advice of the assembly, as colonel and commander in chief of South Carolina forces. One of his duties would be to lead an expedition against Indian enemies, including Yemassees.[446] This is the same John Palmer who in 1715 was described

---

444   BPRO Roll 2 Vol. 10 p. 38/39
445   Hewatt, Alexander *History* 1836 Carroll edition p. 271
446   BPRO Roll 3 Vol. 13 p. 173

as a youth, who with others scaled the walls of the Indian fort.

Palmer gathered together a force of 200, consisting of militia and friendly Indians, and entered Florida with the intent of spreading desolation. When his force arrived at St. Augustine, he killed thirty Yemassees, took fifteen men prisoner, destroyed their crops, drove off their livestock and burned the main Yemassee town. By this expedition, Palmer convinced the Spanish of their weakness and the folly of their policy of having Indians raid South Carolina. Palmer convinced the Spanish that the South Carolinians could raid and destroy Florida at will.[447] Palmer scored an impressive victory, causing the Indians to lose all respect for the Spanish, a respect never regained. The Lower Creeks were so impressed with the victory they immediately made peace with South Carolina on English terms. As a result, South Carolina would know greater security than it had in a decade and a half.[448]

---

447   Hewatt 1836 Carroll edition p. 271
448   Sirmans, Eugene *Colonial South Carolina* p.157 (from Crane *Southern Frontier* 249-51, 271-72)

EFFECTS OF THE YEMASSEE INDIAN WAR

By the end of the War of Spanish Succession in 1713, Florida's population was at its lowest point with perhaps 1,000 people living there. The Yemassee War began the repopulation of Florida. In 1716 and 1717 the Apalachee, refugees from the Yemassee War, received permission to settle south of present Tallahassee. So, some of the Apalachee were able to return to Florida after their forced exile by South Carolina in 1704. The Yemassees fled to locations near St. Augustine. Later the Creek from the Chattahoochee and Flint River districts in present day Georgia and Alabama began pouring into the unpopulated center of Florida.[449]

On the other hand, South Carolina's southern frontier had been devastated and depopulated. In 1720 there were only thirty white inhabitants of Granville County who paid tax. These thirty were the equivalent of what today would be called "head

---

449 Arnade, Charles W. *The New History of Florida* p. 108

of household" and assuming at least four to a family that would mean the white population would have been 120 as opposed to around 400 prior to April 1715. The thirty taxpayers owned only forty-two slaves.[450] In addition, the Indian population in Granville County had fallen from several hundred to virtually zero.

The entire province had felt a crushing blow. The cattle raising business was devastated. Nearly half of the cultivated land was abandoned in 1715 causing a great lack of food in 1716 and 1717. The war reduced the 1715 white population by some 400 families including those who were murdered or fled. Another assessment estimated the number of white men fit to bear arms dropped dramatically. The numerical superiority of the slave to white population was thus increased by the war. Also, the province had acquired a reputation for danger that limited whites coming to South Carolina for more than a decade. The assembly, beginning in 1716, desperately searched for a means to increase the white population. The duty on slaves was increased to £30 in 1717, but still the number of imported slaves rose.[451]

---

450   BPRO Roll 2 Vol. 9 p. 23
451   Jabbs, Theodore *The South Carolina Militia 1663 – 1733* p. 318/319

The war ended South Carolina's policy of relying on friendly Indians to protect its inland borders. Instead, garrisons were built on its frontiers.[452] One such garrison was Fort Moore, built in the winter of 1715 on the east bank of the Savannah River, just south of present Augusta, Georgia. Its purposes were to guard Savano Town, a nearby Indian trading town, and to guard Savano path, the principal route used by the Creeks to travel to Charles Town. The fort, situated on a 200-foot high bluff, was made of wood with its wall only about four and a half feet high. Light cannons were mounted in the bastions in each corner. Living conditions in the fort were terrible with flies plaguing people during the day and mosquitoes during the night. The nearby woods were the latrine. Until the late 1740s, the majority of the soldiers who comprised the forts' garrisons were members of South Carolina's own provincial army. Fort Moore was the most important of South Carolina's early frontier forts.[453]

In addition to the expense of the garrisons, the government decided the province could not burden the volunteers indefinitely and would pay its soldiers. The government even "purchased" soldiers from abroad. The indentures of these servant soldiers ran for seven years, but any soldier could have that

---

452 Ibid. p. 305
453 Ivers, Larry E *Colonial Forts of South Carolina 1670-1775* p. 11/62/63

reduced to four years if he distinguished himself in battle. Some deserted their posts, but most were serving faithfully in the forts at Port Royal and at Fort Moore in December 1717.[454]

The Rev. Francis LeJau wrote many letters. Sometimes he seemed to exaggerate. In his letter of March 18, 1717,[455] he stated 1,500 white men had been lost in the war. This figure is much too high. But he continued in the same letter to give a fairly accurate account of the costs of the war. He stated the merchants from England lost £50,000, a loss caused by the Indians not paying their debts. The province was £90,000 in debt including £30,000 the assembly had issued in 1715 in new bills of credit and an additional £20,000 in 1716. That was more than the province's credit could bear.[456] The large number of South Carolina bills of credit in circulation, which had to be issued to fiancé the war, was causing South Carolina currency to devaluate against the British sterling. LeJau reported an English shilling was worth more than five South Carolina shillings. In 1703 the rate of exchange was 1.5 South Carolina to £1 sterling and by 1718 it had risen to 5 to 1. It leveled off at 7 to 1 by 1726. LeJau complained his annual salary of £100 South Carolina money was

---

454 Jabbs, Theodore *Colonial Militia* p. 310
455 Society for the Propagation of the Gospel microfilm South Carolina Historical Society SPG 296 (958-70-3) p. 70
456 Sirmans, Eugene *Colonial South Carolina* p. 115/116

only worth £18 sterling and he and the rest of the clergy were suffering. All, he continued, were paying great taxes.

The Indian trade changed for a while. An act was enacted June 30, 1716, that would turn the Indian trade into a public monopoly. There were to be three trading "factories." The factories or trading posts were Fort Moore near Savano Town, one near the Congarees and one at Winyah near the Santee River. The Indians would bring their skins to one of these three places. The assembly would pay merchants to purchase items that could be traded with the Indians. Indians were paid to take these goods to the factories and again paid to take the skins to Charles Town. In Charles Town the skins were sold, hopefully at a profit. All involved in the process were paid salaries.

The act provided that anyone who traded illegally with Indians allied with the English would be fined £500 plus forfeiture of any goods. However, the Virginians continued their encroaching and were undercutting the prices of the English. In 1718 a large supply of goods was embezzled. John Sharp, assistant factor to the Cherokees, beat and abused some of these Indians. The commissioners promised he would be punished. In a letter of June 27, 1718, it was reported there were interlopers trading illegally.

Compared to the journals of the Indian commissioners prior to April 12, 1715, these few complaints from July 4, 1716, to August 29, 1718, would seem very mild except to the Indians who were beaten.

The public monopoly raised loud criticism and the Indians complained about long journeys to the factories. The Charles Town merchants were not happy. The people still distrusted the private traders but felt they provided a better and more efficient way than the new reformed way. By 1721 the whole trade was back in private hands.[457]

The most important change that the Yemassee War helped bring about was the Revolution of 1719. It changed South Carolina from a province ruled by eight Lord Proprietors to a royal colony. It was a transition that lasted from 1719 to 1729.

---

457 Wallace, D.D. *South Carolina A Short History* p. 125

POSTLUDE

The Yemassee War was tragic for the white settlers as well as the Indians. Greed, as is often the case, was the real culprit. Regardless of the cause of the war, it was thrust unexpectedly on the province and it had to be fought. South Carolinians fought valiantly with little outside assistance and at great hardship.

The Indians were defeated for several reasons. The main reason was because of the bravery of South Carolina's militia and later its paid soldiers. It was the militia, however, not paid soldiers, who turned the tide in the opening fury. Young Palmer scaling the Indian walls at Pocataligo is a good example of that bravery. The South Carolina militia and soldiers had another advantage in that they were better armed than the Indians. Another factor contributing to the Indian loss was that not all the tribes participated as promised and the Cherokees decided to join with South Carolina. Outside help to South Carolina was very limited, other than the arms and ammunition South Carolina purchased in New England, the arms and ammunition sent from England and the "rented" soldiers from Virginia. None of these was a major factor in defeating the Indians.

Seymour Burrows, a true hero, has been virtually forgotten and deserves to be honored by South Carolina. John Barnwell is remembered for many things, but he is not remembered for his frantic ride in a canoe up the coast to warn settlers of a possible attack. So many did so much to protect South Carolina.

Sometimes our ancestors complained and often they were afraid, but they were, as are we, only human. Most of them did their best and they were successful in the end. Let us remember these brave men, women and children of South Carolina. "Any age can only be judged by its own criteria, not by those of hindsight or posterity."[458]

458 Sinclair-Stevenson, Christopher *Inglorious Rebellion The Jacobite Risings of 1708, 1715 and 1719* p. 15

POST SCRIPT

The identity of the last surviving veteran of the Yemassee War will probably never be known, but a likely guess would be Edward Thomas. He was one of the horsemen who rode into the ambush with Captain Thomas Barker in late May 1715. Edward Thomas was wounded there. He lived about fifty years after the war in St. Stephen's Parish, fifteen of which he never left his plantation. Then he moved to England where he met John Palmer, also of St. Stephen's Parish, and Thomas spoke to Palmer of the Yemassee War.[459]

---

459 Hicks, Theresa M. (Edited by) *South Carolina Indians and Indian Traders* p. 42

BIBLIOGRAPHY

Andrews, William *Old Time Punishments* Williamstown, MA: Corner House Publishers, 1985 Reprinted from the original 1910 copy.

Axtell, James *The Indians' New South* Baton Rouge: Louisiana State University Press, 1997 "Reprinted with permission of the LSU Press."

Barker, Eirlys *Pryce Hughes* South Carolina Historical Society (SCHS) *Magazine* Vol. 95

The *Bible* inspired by God

British Public Records Office (BPRO) available in the South Carolina Room in the Charleston County Library, 68 Calhoun St., Charleston, SC

Burns, E. Radford *"Latin America – A Concise Interpretative History* New York: Prentice Hall 1994

Cheves, Langdon He edited articles about the Yemassee War for the 1894 *City of Charleston Yearbook.*

Crane, Verner W. *The Southern Frontier 1670-1732* Ann Arbor: The University of Michigan Press, 1964

Dodson, Leonidas *Alexander Spotswood – Governor of Colonial Virginia 1710 –* Philadelphia: University of Pennsylvania Press 1932

Edgar, Walter & Bailey, N. Louise *Biographical Directory of the South Carolina House of Representatives Vol. II* Columbia: University of South Carolina Press, 1977

Fagg, Daniel W. Jr. *St. Giles: The Earl of Shaftesbury's Carolina Plantation* SCHS *Magazine* Vol. 71

Fraser, Walter J. *Charleston, Charleston* Columbia: University of South Carolina Press, 1989

Gannon, Michael who edited *The New History of Florida* Gainesville, FL: University Press of Florida, 1996. Excerpts were used from chapters written by Charles W. Arnade, Amy Turner Buswell and John H. Hann. "Reprinted with permission of the University Press of Florida."

Giraud, Marcel *A History of French Louisiana 1698 – 1715* Baton Rouge & London: Louisiana State University Press, second printing 1990. Translated from French by Joseph C. Lambert "Reprinted with permission from LSU Press."

Goodman, Paul "Essays in American Colonial History" New York: Holt, Rinehart & Winston 1967

Hewatt, Alexander *Historical Collections of South Carolina ... compiled with various notes and an introduction by B.R. Carroll* New York, NY: Harper & Brothers, 1836.

Hicks, Theresa M. who edited *South Carolina Indians and Indian* Traders Spartanburg: Published for Peppercorn Publications, Inc. by The Reprint Company Publishers, 1998

Higginbotham, Jay *Old Mobile – Fort Louis de la Louisiane 1702 – 1711* Mobile: Museum of the City of Mobile, 1977 "Reprinted with permission from the author."

Holcombe, Brent H *South Carolina Marriages 1688-1799* Baltimore: Genealogical Publishing Co. Inc. 1983

Ivers, Larry *The Yemassee War in the Beaufort and Port Royal area* Unpublished. Also SCHS *Magazine* Vol. 73 *Scouting the Inland Passage 1685-1737. Also Colonial Forts of South Carolina.*

Jabbs, Theodore *The South Carolina Colonial Militia 1663-1773* Ann Arbor: U.M.I. Dissertation Services, 1993. A PhD dissertation in 1973 at the University of North Carolina at Chapel Hill

Johnson, Capt. Charles H. *A General History of the Robberies & Murders of the Most Notorious Pirates* The Lyons Press

Johnson, David Lee *The Yamasee War* Submitted in partial fulfillment of the requirements for the Degree of Master of Arts in the Department of History University of South Carolina 1980. This work can be found at the Thomas Cooper Library at the University of South Carolina.

King, Grace & Ficklen, John R. *History of Louisiana* New Orleans: L. Graham & Sons, 1893

Kirk, Francis Marion *The Yamassee War* Unpublished

Leckie, Robert *The Wars of America* New York: Harper Perennial – a Division of Harper Collins Publisher, 1993

Lee, Charles E. & Green, Ruth S. who edited *A Guide to the Commons House Journal of the South Carolina General Assembly 1692-1721*. These are called the *Green Journals* and are available at the South Carolina Archives in Columbia.

Lefler, Hugh Talmage edited by and introduction to *A New Voyage to Carolina* by John Lawson. Chapel Hill, NC: The University of North Carolina Press, 1967

Lefler, Hugh Talmage & Powell, William S. *Colonial North Carolina* New York: Charles Scribner's Sons 1973

MacDougal, Margaret O. & Barn, Robert *Clans & Tartans of Scotland*

Marks, Geoffrey & Beaty, William K. *The Story of Medicine in America* New York: Charles Scribner's Sons

McCord, David *Statues At Large of South Carolina 1682-1716 Vol. II* Columbia: A. S. Johnson, 1837

McCrady, Edward *History of South Carolina 1670 - 1719* New York: Russell & Russell 1897, reprinted by Russell & Russell in 1969.

McDowell, W. L. Jr., edited *Journals of the Commissioners of the Indian Trade* Columbia: South Carolina Department of Archives & History, 1992

Moore, Alexander edited by and introduction to *Nairne's Muskhogean Journals The 1708 Expedition to the Mississippi River* Jackson and London: University Press of Mississippi, 1988. "Reprinted with permission of University Press of Mississippi and the author."

Morton, Richard L. *Colonial Virginia Vol. II* Chapel Hill: Published for the Virginia Historical Society by the University of North Carolina Press, 1960

Otto, John S. *The Origins of Cattle-Raising in Colonial South Carolina 1670-1715* SCHS *Magazine* Vol. 87

Palmer, William P edited Vol. 1 *Calendar of State Papers (Virginia)* Richmond: "arranged, edited and printed under the authority and direction of H.W. Flournoy, Secretary of the Commonwealth and State Librarian." 1875

Phillips, G.R. *Charleston's Past* Post & Courier April 4, 2002 p. 2ZB

Raimo, John W. *Biographical Directory of American and Colonial & Revolutionary Governors 1607-1789* Westport: Meckler Books – a division of Microform Review, 1980

Ramsey, William L. SCHS *Magazine* Vol. 103

Rowland, Dunbar & Sanders, Albert G. *Mississippi Provincial Archives 1704-1743* Jackson: Press of the Mississippi Department of Archives and History 1932

Salley, A.S. edited *Journals of the Common House of the Assembly*

Salley, A.S. edited *Warrants for Lands in South Carolina* Columbia: Printed for The Historical Commission of South Carolina by The State Co., 1910. Reprinted, three volumes in one, for Clearfield Co. Inc. by Genealogical Publishing Co., Inc. Baltimore, 1992.

Sinclair-Stevenson, Christopher *Inglorious Rebellion-The Jacobite Risings of 1708, 1715 & 1719* London: Hamish Hamilton 1971

Sirmans, Eugene *Colonial South Carolina: a political history 1663 - 1763* Raleigh: University of North Carolina Press, 1966

Smith, Henry Augustus Middleton *Historical Writings of Henry A.M. Smith Vol. II Cities & Towns of South Carolina* Published in association with the South Carolina Historical Society Spartanburg: the Reprint Company, Publisher 1988

Snell, William R *Indian Slavery in South Carolina 1671-1795* Ann Arbor: U.M.I. Dissertation Services, 1993. A 1973 dissertation at the University of Alabama.

Society for the Propagation of the Gospel in Foreign Parts (SPG). Microfiche is available at the South Carolina Historical Society, 100 Meeting Street, Charleston, South Carolina 29401.

Todd, John R. & Hutson, Francis M *Prince William's Parish & Plantations* Richmond: Garrett & Massie, 1935 Introduction by A.S. Salley.

Waddell, Gene, *Indians of the South Carolina Lowcountry 1562-1751* Spartanburg: the Reprint Company, Publishers, 1980

Wallace, D.D. *South Carolina – A Short History* Chapel Hill: The University of North Carolina Press, 1951

Waring, J. I. *Story of Medicine in South Carolina 1670-1825* Columbia: R. L. Bryant Co, 1964. Copyrighted in 1964 by the South Carolina Medical Association. Reprinted by the Reprint Company, Publishers in Spartanburg.

White, John Manchip *Everyday Life of the North American Indian* New York: Dorset Press a division of Marboro Books Corp, 1988 "Permission to reprint given by the author."

Whitney, Edson *Government of the Colony of South Carolina* Baltimore: The John Hopkin's Press, 1895

INDEX

Trott, Nicholas 53
Tynte, Edward 109

Vanvelsin, Garrett 104

Wansella 45
Warner, Samuel 94, 96
Wateree 150
Welch, Thomas 69–71
Westbrook, Caleb 8
Wenoya 90
Wettly 241
Whitehead, John 85
Wiatt, Steven 121
Wigg, Richard 202, 203, 205–207

Wiggan, Eleazer 171, 182, 185
Wiggasay 46
Wigington, Henry 92
Williams, James 157
Woodward, Henry 11–15, 220
Woodward, John 97, 110
Woodward, Richard 110
Wright, John 44, 47, 96, 97

Yeamans, John 12
Yonge, Francis 96

Zendoya 221
Zuniga, Joseph 222

4752790R0

Made in the USA
Charleston, SC
11 March 2010